Public/Private Partnerships for Local Governments

Oliver W. Porter

authorHOUSE®

AuthorHouse™
1663 Liberty Drive, Suite 200
Bloomington, IN 47403
www.authorhouse.com
Phone: 1-800-839-8640

First published by AuthorHouse 10/2/2008

ISBN: 978-1-4343-9836-9 (sc)
ISBN: 978-1-4343-9837-6 (hc)

Library of Congress Control Number: 2008907745

Printed in the United States of America
Bloomington, Indiana

This book is printed on acid-free paper.

ABOUT the AUTHOR

Oliver W. Porter has become a leading proponent of the value of Public/Private partnerships to local governments. Mr. Porter's involvement with this subject and his development of a new model for providing municipal services began with the community, now city, of Sandy Springs, Georgia. In January, 2005, he accepted the challenge of implementing the first new city in Georgia in fifty years; a city that would serve 90,000 citizens, the seventh largest city in the state, at birth. The challenge was made extremely difficult by the fact that he, nor anyone else, would have any funds, staff or authority prior to the incorporation date for the city. Working as the volunteer Interim City Manager, Oliver Porter recruited and organized the other volunteers to perform the data gathering and analysis necessary to understand the needs and financial capability of the new city. Recognizing that under the constraints with which he dealt, it would not be possible to start the city using traditional methods for providing services, he proposed a new model to the community. After selling his concept of a Public/Private partnership, he moved in only a few months to actually bring the concept to reality. During that period, Mr. Porter also served as the Chairman of an advisory group, the Governor's Commission on Sandy Springs. Upon the successful implementation of the city, Mr. Porter served the city for four months as a transition consultant. During this period he wrote his first book, *Creating the New City of Sandy Springs; The 21st Century Paradigm: Private Industry.* The book has served as a very useful guide for other new cities, particularly those that were interested in the new model.

The value of the Sandy Springs model is confirmed by the actions of other communities in the state. In the two years following the incorporation of Sandy Springs, three new cities have followed suit. All three have embraced the model created by Mr. Porter, and he has served as the principal advisor to all. The state legislature has just authorized a referendum on the creation of a fifth city. Oliver Porter has been selected to serve again as the advisor and it is expected that the Public/Private partnership model will be given strong consideration.

The local metropolitan newspaper has published articles referring to Mr. Porter as the "Incorporation Guru", the "Metro Maestro" and "Father of Cities" in reporting his activities on behalf of local governments.

After publication of his first book, Mr. Porter has provided advice and assistance to a number of communities and existing cities across America.

Very recently his influence was extended to the international scene when he was invited under a grant by the Ministry of Education and Finance of Japan to participate in a series of symposia and meetings with leaders of government, business and academia in that country. It appears very possible that several Japanese cities may begin conversion to the Public/Private partnership model.

Given the above, the reader might assume that Oliver Porter's background was in the area of Government. Actually, nothing could be further from the truth. Possibly the lack of a background in government enhanced Mr. Porter's ability to "think out of the box" in seeking new methods for providing services. A native of South Carolina, Mr. Porter attended the University of South Carolina on a naval ROTC scholarship. Graduating in the top ten percent of his class, with a degree in Civil Engineering, he was a member of Tau Beta Pi, engineering honor society, and the president of Pi Kappa Alpha fraternity. Upon graduation he served for three years as an officer in the U.S. Navy. Resigning his commission,

Mr. Porter entered the corporate world as an engineer with Southern Bell Telephone. He attained the status of a Registered Professional Engineer in South Carolina and earned an MBA at Georgia State University, where he was again in the top ten percent of his class and inducted into Beta Gamma Sigma, honor society for management. Moving rapidly through a number of positions of increasing responsibility in engineering, planning, finance and marketing he chose to transfer to AT&T at the time of the splitting up of the Bell System. He set up and managed the fourteen state Southern Region for General Business Markets, retiring as Vice President of sales in 1989.

During his corporate career and in subsequent years Oliver Porter has been very active in charitable affairs. He served as the National Chairman of two major health organizations – the National Kidney Foundation and the Combined Health Appeal of America. He was the founding leader of the latter organization as he was for two state charities. Over the years Mr. Porter founded, or served as the catalyst for, over a dozen state and metropolitan health charities. He also has been instrumental in the establishment of churches in a number of locations. Pursuing his interest in painting during retirement, Oliver Porter has become an artist and has served as the Chairman of Georgia's largest art club and a board member of the Foundation for Hospital Art. All of this corporate and charitable organizational experience was valuable in his efforts to create a new model for local government.

Recently Mr. Porter has been named a Research fellow by Georgia Tech and is advising on a study comparing Public/Private partnerships with comparable traditionally managed cities.

In addition to all of the above activities, Oliver Porter is an avid pursuer of physical fitness. He enjoys the distinction of being the only person who can claim to have run the first Peachtree Road Race, a 10K event with over 55,000 participants; peddled the BRAG, a 400 plus mile bike ride across Georgia, and paddled in the first 'Canoe Across Georgia'. Mr. Porter believes that these accomplishments may point more to his stamina than his intelligence.

Married for 49 years with children and grandchildren, Oliver Porter has enjoyed a full life. Corporate executive, charitable leader, implementer of cities, entrepreneur, scholar, athlete, artist and author, he has been often referred to as a "renaissance man".

In response to the increasing interest in Public/Private partnerships across America, and now in Japan, Oliver Porter has written this second book which recommends the application of the Public/Private partnership concept for existing cities.

ACKNOWLEDGEMENTS

Jeffrey Lee Satterfield

The contribution to the publication of this book by Jeffrey Lee Satterfield must be gratefully acknowledged. Jeff is a published novelist with great editing skills, and has corrected an embarrassing number of mistakes and grammar in my original text, while suggesting improved phraseology.

A number of public officials contributed important comments on the results achieved through the use of Public/Private partnerships in their respective cities. With appreciation, in order of appearance, to:

Mayor Eva Galambos,	Sandy Springs, Georgia
Mayor Joe Lockwood,	Milton, Georgia
Mayor Mike Bodker,	Johns Creek, Georgia
Tom Reed, Organizer	Chattahoochee Hill Country, Georgia
John McDonough,	City Manager Sandy Springs, Georgia

DEDICATION

To the millions of citizens of local governments who are not receiving the efficient and responsive services that they deserve.

PREFACE

Two years have elapsed since the incorporation of the new city of Sandy Springs, Georgia. The process of implementing the city in a very short number of months against long odds was described in my book titled: "*Creating the New City of Sandy Springs*"; "*The 21st Century Paradigm: Private Industry*". Since that time, there have been a number of requests to produce a follow up book that:

(1) describes the results of our unorthodox approach to government services, and

(2) expands on the subject of the use of private industry.

The latter interest flows from existing cities that are concerned that traditional methods for providing local government services are, at best, less than optimal; or, in some cases failing.

The intent of this sequel is to build on the experience of the last two years, in considering the potential opportunity presented by the Public/Private partnership model for existing traditional cities.

Since this is a new concept for some, let us begin by defining several important terms. For the purpose of this book:

Traditional city:

A city in which the majority of core functions/services are provided by city employees.

Core services

A set of functions/services necessary for conducting business in the majority of cities. These functions include:
- Administration
- Accounting
- Finance
- Human Resources
- IT (Information Technology)
- Support (record keeping, communications, systems, processing) for:
    - Police
    - Fire
    - Courts
- Community Development
- Transportation
- Parks/Recreation
- Public works

Non core services

A set of services that typically may be provided internally, contracted, or outsourced in Traditional cities. These include: that includes:

- Capital projects
- Enterprise functions
- Public safety
- Libraries
- Health and Welfare
- Utilities

Capital projects

Functions that are funded outside the annual operating budget, often the provision of major fixed assets,

Enterprise functions

Operations that are financed and operated in a manner similar to business enterprises. Public utilities are a common example.

Public safety

Operations of:
Police
Fire,
EMS
E911
Courts

Public/Private partnerships, or P/P/P

Cities that provide the preponderance of core functions/services via contracts with private industry. (sometimes referred to as the Sandy Springs model in this book)..
For this purpose, "preponderance" means 90% or higher

Sandy Springs Model

The most extensive application of a Public/Private partnership in local government to date.

Privatization

The sale of city (public) assets to a private company.

Other terms that may be useful:

Business Systems – A set of standard practices and protocols that support effective, successful operations.

City Manager – Senior administrative official in a city government who oversees day-to-day activities and citizen services. The city Manager may direct the services of the private partner and related service providers. Reports to the Mayor and City Council.

City Services also Municipal Services – Any of a group of specialized contract services delivered to a city government by a private entity. Services may include, but are not limited to, staffing, communications, public information, accounting, plan review, code enforcement, street and right-of-way maintenance, public works, traffic and transportation engineering, planning, and parks and recreation.

Community Development – Planning, zoning, plan-review, and permitting/code enforcement functions performed by a city government. Also may be known by other similar terms such as Development Services, Land Development, or Land Use.

Contract City – A municipal government that partners with the private sector for the delivery of its services to citizens.

Contracting and Agreement Structures – The business arrangements under which operating partnerships are developed. Agreement types may include lump sum, fixed fee, time and materials, and cost-plus-service fees.

Incorporation – Carrying out a decision to form a municipal government and begin operating as a city.

Performance Metrics – The standards by which clients evaluate the services they receive from a service provider or similar outsourcing partner.

Quality Management – The practice of standardizing, measuring and improving the overall performance of a service, product, or organization.

Referendum Vote – The practice of submitting a measure passed by a legislative body or popular initiative to a vote of the people.

Request for Proposals (RFP) – A formal document, issued by a buyer of services such as a city government, that solicits a price and a procurement/performance approach for a desired group of products or services.

Request for Qualifications (RFQ) – A formal document, issued by a buyer of services such as a city government, which requires respondents to describe their abilities and experience. Statements of qualification in response to RFQs may include information about similar services performed previously, credentials of proposed staff, work approach, and operating philosophy.

Revenue Enhancement – A specialized license-fee collection and taxing service for municipalities on a consulting/contingency basis. License fees and local taxes collected from businesses and professionals operating in the community are an important source of a city's revenue stream.

Risk Allocation/Risk Sharing –The pre-agreed portion of loss or hazard potential, financial or otherwise, assumed by each party in a partnership or business agreement.

Startup and Implementation – A sequence of activities and events, executed according to a prearranged schedule, that culminate in the initiation and ongoing delivery of services such as municipal operations.

Startup Team – A group of functional experts that organizes and coordinates key components of the startup and implementation. Startup team members may be experts in administration, technical services, finance, staffing and personnel, operations, and compliance.

Total Outsourcing – A business arrangement under which a company provides specialized services, technologies, or products for another company or public agency with the goal of managing costs and enhancing efficiency.

TABLE OF CONTENTS

CHAPTER I

"History is the interpretation of the significance that the
past has for us"
-Johan Huizinga

RECENT HISTORY

Since the formation of the new city of Sandy Springs on December 1, 2005, three more new cities have been incorporated in Georgia. The cities of Johns Creek (population 62,000) and Milton (20,000) were established on December 1, 2006. Chattahoochee Hill Country (3,000) became the fourth and latest new city on December1, 2007. The author served as the principal advisor during the implementation phase for all three cities.

All the new cities chose to adopt a Public/Private partnership(i.e., the Sandy Springs model). In that model, in addition to the core services being provided by private industry, there is one company responsible for managing and coordinating all the core functions.

Most governments have contracts with private companies to provide specific services. This is commonly referred to as "outsourcing". The Sandy Springs model goes well beyond outsourcing, in that it offers a broader scope of management. Both the range of services and the management responsibility are greater in the Sandy Springs model.

A number of subcontractors are included under the umbrella of the management company

Given the proximity of the new cities to Sandy Springs and their opportunity for an intimate knowledge of the financial and service benefits accruing to Sandy Springs, their decision is a strong testimony to the perceived benefits of the Public/Private partnership model.

There is a strong possibility that a fifth city, Dunwoody (pop. 40,000) will be formed in 2008. The bill to authorize a referendum on incorporation has just been signed into law, and provides for a referendum of the citizens that is expected to take place on July 15, 2008. If the referendum receives a favorable vote the city of Dunwoody will be incorporated on December 1, 2008. At this point, the organizing committee is very interested in considering the Sandy Springs model. The author has been heavily involved with the organizers and is convinced that a Public/Private partnership will be the best method for providing services to Dunwoody.

In all the new cities in Georgia, the core services are provided by the same company: CH2MHill. While other firms competed for the contracts, CH2MHill emerged as the clear choice for the job. The subsequent performance of the company has validated their selection.

At the beginning of 2005, when we began to develop the Public/Private partnership option for serving Sandy Springs, the author wrote to two dozen major national and international firms. Each was asked two questions:

(1) Where have you provided any of twelve core services needed by our government?

(2) Would you be willing to invest the necessary funds ($ millions) to set up the city without a contract?

Several firms were able to identify services that had been provided to local governments. Most companies deftly evaded the second question on establishing services before a contract could be awarded. CH2MHill agreed to that condition; and, after a thorough evaluation process, was selected for the job. Their performance in Sandy Springs positioned them as the leading contender for the subsequent cities' contracts.

Currently, although a number of firms have the capability to provide local government services, Ch2MHill by its willingness to take a risk, and by virtue of the recent contracts, positioned itself as the leading provider of Public/Private partnerships with local governments.

Before leaving this section, the difference between a Public/Private partnership, Outsourcing and Privatization should be clearly understood.

As defined in the preface, Privatization involves the actual sale, or long term lease, of city property. There is no transfer of property under the Public/Private partnership model, which is a services contract.

Outsourcing, for the purposes of this book, is the act of contracting a service, or services, to a private firm, while the management of the city as a whole remains under city employees and the majority of core services is provided by city employees.

In contrast, the Sandy Springs Model of P/P/P places the provision of the majority of public services under a management contract with private industry.

CHAPTER II

...to give him the benefits of a government that could have promoted the enterprise and furnished the convenience and the facilities needed by every man, woman and child in this country

-Huey Long

BENEFITS

Among the benefits that the Public/Private partnership cities are experiencing are:

LOWER COSTS and BETTER SERVICE through:

* Greater efficiencies
* Synergies
* Cost sharing
    Intracity
    Intercity
* Flexibility
* Outside resources
* Reduced liabilities
* Improved contract management
* Quality employees
* Expedited decision processes

Contacts with any of the Public/Private Partnership cities can verify these benefits.

The city of Sandy Springs has been operational for two years. Mayor Eva Galambos, who was the prime mover in starting the city for over two decades, has had the best opportunity of anyone in the nation to evaluate the advantages or disadvantages of the Public/Private partnership that we have come to call the Sandy Springs model. Following is a quote from Mayor Galambos:

> *Sandy Springs has had a very satisfactory experience during the last two years with our public-private partnership. First of all, we could never have started all the administrative elements of managing a city of 90,000 population with a budget of $79 million without the efficiency of the private sector. Their ability to subcontract with other private entities that could immediately provide us with the vast array of computer programs, financial and accounting systems, human relations management and all the other aspects of administration from day one was essential to our successful startup. The ability of the private sector to move quickly, without the many encumbrances on rapid purchasing in the public arena, definitely contributed to this successful beginning.Yet the profit motive of the private company that runs most of our services provides the discipline to keep the cost of these subcontracts low.*
>
> *As we have progressed past startup, we continue to be pleased with the efficiencies of the private sector. A comparison of the number of employees, including those of the private company, against neighboring municipalities shows that our partnership arrangement entails fewer people. That of course provides ultimate savings.*
>
> *Our contract with the private company is for a fixed sum annually, with a cost of living escalation, for a described array of services. Our City Manager is an employee of the City, and the ultimate executive officer over the entire operation, including the departments of the City that are staffed with the employees of the private provider. This arrangement calls for a great deal of finesse and ingenuity. Our City Manager does not have the ultimate right to hire or fire*

the employees of the Company, but definitely communicates his evaluation of their performance to the Company.
The City Manager monitors if there are unfilled vacancies in departments for which the Company is responsible under the contract. If the vacancies are not filled in a timely manner, the City Manager relays this information to the Company . Ultimately the City may withhold payment to the Company if a vacancy remains unfilled too long, but in order to make the relationship work, the two parties expend major efforts to communicate and be open about any problems.

A great deal of the success of our plan depends on the ability of the two parties to be open with each other, and to work out any problems that may arise. To some extent this is dependent on the personalities involved. Our City Manager came on board knowing that this would entail a totally different approach to government, and he embraced the opportunity to be a part of this process.This is a major contributor to the success of our joint venture. Several Council Members as well as I were involved in the effort to create the City of Sandy Springs and were parties to the original decision to involve the private sector to the greatest possible extent. The entire Council has been supportive of the arrangement and anxious to make it work. Council has delineated some issues on which they would like further communication with the Company, and a committee of the Council will meet with Company representatives to delve into the items. Mostly they do not involve any shortcomings of currently provided services. Instead they seek cutting edge ideas on even more progressive service delivery options. An example is a request to the Company to provide us with options to expedite capital improvement projects, with possible combination of design and build components.

In conclusion, at this stage I highly recommend our approach to this public/private delivery of local government services.

The leaders of other cities will be quoted throughout this material. Each will speak from the viewpoint of their own community; but, in general, all are supportive of the benefits to be derived from Public/Private partnerships.

The author asserts the existence of these benefits, based on his experience and observation of the new city governments. Let us expand on the points listed above.

A. EFFICIENCIES

Many Traditional cities have fallen victim to decades of inefficient processes and lack of employee productivity, sometimes as a result of coercion by unions and/or weariness with battling civil service type regulations. For whatever reason, a pattern of less than optimal efficiency and poorer than necessary public service is pervasive. The local governments certainly cannot look to the federal and state governments to provide better examples. Government at all levels in this country is bloated. Logjammed by over a hundred years of bad practices in a vicious cycle of more government, higher taxes, more government, on and on, the trend has continued.

Let me say, up front, that many city employees are both talented and hard working. The problem is the antiquated system in which they are forced to operate.

Basically, inertia has resulted from all those years of doing business the same way. Cities have become inefficient employers. Some employees have learned to do only that which is required to keep their jobs (and that it is so much of a legal hassle to fire them, that it is rarely done!) The system promotes a "not my job" attitude that citizens so often encounter in any government dealings. There is little incentive to innovate or to be more than minimally productive.

Against this backdrop, private industry has little challenge in producing better results.

The tools that industry brings to the task are many and varied.

1. Incentives

Normal incentives for employee performance, would include: pay, promotion, a feeling of accomplishment, and fear of job loss. For the employee in many Traditional cities, most, if not all of these factors are squelched. By comparison, private industry tends to offer better compensation and more opportunities to advance. For example, a company can offer advancement opportunities in locations not limited to the current city. In the corporate setting there is more encouragement and opportunity to innovate.

A reader's question might be "if industry offers more pay, how can it cut costs"? The direct answer is: through **improved productivity**. The roots of this improvement will be covered in detail.

To believe that employee attitude is not different under these two disparate models, Traditional and Private, is to believe in the tooth fairy. The author has observed both models in action and does not have faith in the tooth fairy. The clear fact is that the new Public/Private partnership cities are performing specific service functions with substantially fewer employees than are required in comparable Traditional cities, while simultaneously producing superior service.

2. Complacency

One of the charges most frequently leveled against Traditional city employees is their complacency. Citizens are frustrated by the "not my job" attitude so pervasive at all levels of government. Let me cite one very frustrating contact with the IRS as an example of government run around.

When I was the volunteer chairman of a national health charity, I called the IRS to determine the status of a state affiliate's 501(c)(3) tax exemption application. I was referred to seven consecutive staffers, before I arrived back at the original person!

Unfortunately, such occurrences are common for citizens contacting with their local governments. This type performance has not been a part of the history of Public/Private partnerships and will not be tolerated by a firm with a strong profit motive.

Employee attitude is only one part of the efficiency equation. The other component is having the most effective tools for the job; i.e., equipment, systems, training, methodology, etc. Industry is far superior at providing these elements that drive productivity.

3. Innovation

Innovation is the life's blood of a Public/Private partnership. Traditional cities have difficulty with true innovation. Change has tended to be incremental and slow. The new Public/Private Partnership cities have thrived on innovation. Some examples will be provided later. For now, it should be obvious that better compensation incentives, promotion opportunities, and work environments conducive to creativity, do result in more innovative approaches.

Finally, although it is a negative influencer, the concern about holding on to one's job can be an important factor. Traditional cities are burdened with many employees who are "dead wood". Through painful experience, cities are well aware of the difficulty in firing poor performers. Supervisors have often given up due to the regulations and legal obstacles to dismissing, or even disciplining, weak employees.

Private firms can, and do, step up to this difficult job.

Employees who know that their company's contract with the city, and therefore their own jobs, depend on performance have ample incentive to produce service that is satisfying to the citizens.

Many examples of innovation have been introduced under the P/P/P model. Some will be described in later sections of this book. Two short examples that do not fall under other topics may be appropriate to mention at this time.

Before the new P/P/P cities were actually operative, the company, CH2MHill, performed an initial condition assessment of every foot of the over five hundred miles of roads, gutters and sidewalks in the communities. The technology that permitted such an exhaustive inventory was a new method of truck mounted LASER cameras. The data that was acquired was downloaded into software that analyzed, evaluated and recorded the condition of the assets. This knowledge, in turn, was used as the basis for constructing the on-going maintenance and capital improvement programs for the city. Thus, even before the cities were in operation, they had a better understanding of the physical transportation needs than had been available in the past.

A second brief example occurred on the revenue side of the ledger. Normally when one thinks of efficiency, the mind turns to a reduction of costs; but revenue increases are also of great importance. In the case of Sandy Springs and the other new cities, when the county government's records were transferred it appeared that the county may have been had very inefficient in the levying and collection of occupational and business licenses. The company set up a revenue enhancement operation to address the perceived revenue loss. A field crew equipped with hand held PDA's was dispatched to canvas all commercial buildings, data about every business was entered and then downloaded at the end of the day to the city's Geographic Information System, where it was compared to the county's database. This process uncovered twice as many businesses as had been on record, and resulting in $2 million in additional revenue to the city, at no incremental cost to the city! Additionally, an ongoing review process has been established to insure that a continuing update will provide correct licensing and revenue in the future.

4. Pay

Returning to the issue of compensation: while nationwide, state and local government employees earn more than private sector employees ($40 versus $26 per hour), the private industry service provider in the Sandy Springs model has tended to pay individuals more than the local scale for government workers. In spite, and in part because, of these higher wages, the overall cost has been lower. The obvious reason is the improved productivity that has more than compensated for the higher wages.

5. Satisfaction

Overriding all of the above is the fact that it is simply more enjoyable to work in an atmosphere of innovation and high performance. It is possible that some of the exceptional enthusiasm seen in the first years after introducing the Sandy Springs model could wane, but there is no indication of that as yet.

We expect that quality employees, seeing the good result of their work, will continue to draw satisfaction from innovation.

6. Improved Contract Management

Cities have significant resources devoted to purchasing functions. In addition, many cities incur substantial expenditure for contracts with private companies and other governments, outside of the core functions/ services. Substantial city resources may be tied up in issuing RFP's, contract evaluation and negotiation, and in managing the contracts.

In Public/Private Partnerships, the purchasing and contracting functions are taken over by the company. Any firm with the capability of managing a P/P/P city will certainly have substantial experience in the areas of purchasing and contract management. These functions lend themselves readily to cost sharing. The required expertise can be called upon when needed and focused elsewhere when not required. This capability allows for a very high level of competency while minimizing costs.

One may certainly posit that there should be no one more knowledgeable in contract negotiation with industry than firms who have themselves been contractors.

7. Expedited Decision Processes

It may be only a reflection of the fewer employees in Public/Private partnerships, but the author observes that decisions occur with less delay than is evident in Traditional cities. Certainly a streamlined chain of command tends to encourage a faster decision-making process. Another factor is reducing departmentalization. Add the profit motive to the equation, and the concept that "time is money", and we may understand the motivation to expedite the decision process.

8. Quality of Employees

A concern in existing cites that are considering the Public/Private partnership model may be the future of current city employees. While this is a legitimate concern, it should be secondary to the need to assure that the city is served by high quality employees.

Over the recent decades, American industry workers have experienced a reduction in long term job security as technology and globalization have exerted a major influence on the workplace. No longer do employees receive, or expect, lifetime jobs with one company. It is time that government begin to recognize this changed environment.

Elected officials owe it to the citizens to seek the most efficient method for providing services and the most productive work force.

So what has been the experience in the P/P/P cities?

(1) They have significantly fewer personnel devoted to providing services than in Traditional cities.

(2) This reduced workforce is producing superior service, and therefore, must be considered to be more productive.

The Public/Private Partnership personnel have been drawn from a number of sources:

(1) At the production level and the first level of supervision, the majority of employees have been drawn from other local

governments.

(2) Senior management has been a mixture of company and local government personnel.

It must be understood that the use of "local government personnel" should not be interpreted as a one-for-one substitution of people. The Public Private Partnerships, due to the factors of better compensation and job satisfaction explained earlier, have been able to select better employees. In a city considering conversion to the P/P/P model, it is to be expected that a similar process will occur. The best employees will obtain good positions in the new model. In many cases, these new positions will be far more rewarding than the old jobs. Additional employees will be drawn from other local governments in the area, i.e. county or state employees. Some new employees may come from industry when their skill sets are required.

In short, the city should enjoy a significant upgrade in personnel.

It may seem hard, but employees who have not been performing well, for whatever reasons, should not be retained by the city. It is time that government officials recognize their responsibility to the citizens to make the tough decisions.

Some people question whether it is possible to terminate all the cities employees, given labor contracts and civil service constraints. The author is neither a labor relations expert nor a lawyer, but offers the following for consideration: The city is not replacing people in jobs; rather, the jobs are being eliminated. Unless the city has allowed itself to be coerced into a labor contract that prohibits job elimination, the process should be legal. If legal, then all that is required is political fortitude.

If contractual constraints exist on job elimination, the city should make it a priority to begin to work toward changing the labor contracts as soon as possible.

The job of city officials is to provide good government, not to be a job provider.

Joe Lockwood is the Mayor of Milton, Georgia, a new city of approximately 20,000 population that was incorporated in December, 2006. Milton opted to establish city services with a Public/Private partnership. Currently, the city employs only five people, in addition to the police and fire departments. During the first year of city-hood, Milton has experienced all the growing pains that can be expected when a new council is elected with relatively inexperienced members who have very different views on such matters as growth and development. Mayor Lockwood has been a steadying influence for the city in its infancy. One of the points that he makes is:

> *Although there has been some turmoil in the political arena, the community is far better served than it was before incorporation. The citizens have an opportunity to speak and be heard that was never present before".*

A second point he offers is that:

> *Having a Public/Private partnership has been far better than trying to start a city from scratch. He referred to the advantages of having access to people with experience and training; and, also, the existing infrastructure that the company (in this case CH2MHill) was able to provide.*

Mayor Lockwood recognized that as complex as the task was of starting a new city, the job would have been infinitely more difficult if there had been a necessity to hire and train new employees, while simultaneously acquiring systems and facilities.

With over a year of operations behind him, the Mayor says:

Obviously, there are advantages and disadvantages to the partnership. However, the advantages have far outweighed the disadvantages.

He continued:

Among the advantages, in addition to the immediately available cadre of competent and enthusiastic workers, were already tested systems that could be quickly adapted to our needs.

There was financial depth that provided assurance during our early period of limited revenue.

The profit motive of the private company seemed to encourage and motivate superior employee attitudes. They seem to work harder and more efficiently.

There were certain services in which we could benefit from sharing resources with other cities and even with the company's other business areas.

And, of course, we were benefiting from the experience that the company was gaining through other cities

In my opinion, the cost-effectiveness of a motivated employee force and shared resources more than offsets the profit margin that the company enjoys.

Basically, we are buying a level of service. If we are not satisfied, we tell the company to fix it; and they make the personnel or organizational changes that are necessary.

When there are short term crises, the company moves in the resources to solve the problem and then removes them. The city is relieved of the burden of hiring, training and then having to try to terminate employees. In other words, the company shoulders much of the risk.

Finally, the most important factor may be the elimination of the long term liability for pension and other benefits that plague many cities and other governments.

The Mayor also spoke to a potential disadvantage that may occur under Public/Private partnerships.

> *I worry that employees may feel torn between working for the company and the city. They must remember that neither organization will do well unless the citizens see them as city employees. I do not think that this is a big problem at present, and it certainly does not outweigh the advantages.*

B. SYNERGIES

A major problem with Traditional cities is the over departmentalization of functions and inflexible use of resources. We have already touched on the problem that employees slotted into one area tend not to be moved between departments, thereby inhibiting their professional growth and/or negatively effecting attitudes. Now consider the effect of departmentalization on efficiency as a whole.

Traditional cities tend to build budgets on the departmental basis. Often on a "last years budget plus X percent" basis. Consider the effect. If department A introduces an innovative program that reduces costs, or manages to increase productivity so as to decrease expenditures, it will likely be "rewarded" with a decrease in the next year's budget ! Not much of an incentive to departmental management.

Private industry, with a greater advantage in incentive weapons such as profit sharing, bonuses, promotional opportunities, employee stock ownership, etc., has the ability to reward the employees who add value to the city as a whole.

When a manager cuts costs his department, the company's profits are increased. When profits increase, good things tend to happen for those responsible.

As an alternative to cutting costs, a manager may improve service at the same cost level. In that case, the company benefits by being better able to hold on to the contract, and again, has the ability to reward those generating the improvement.

Over-departmentalization reduces the incentive for cross department synergies. For example, one department may opt for a system that enhances productivity for its area of responsibility with total disregard for the effect on the whole. The proposed system may actually be detrimental to, or incompatible with, another department.
In effect, departmental managers absent the profit motive and in competition for resources, are not positioned as partners but as competitors. With each department focused on maximizing only one segment of the city, it is little wonder that the overall opportunity for improving efficiency is not being seized.

In the Sandy Springs model, the profit motive serves to focus management on the overall effectiveness, penetrating the departmental walls.

This focus is affirmed By Mayor Mike Bodker of Johns Creek, another Public/Private partnership city. Mayor Bodker led the effort to gain incorporation for the new city of Johns Creek, Georgia, (population 62,000). He was elected as the first Mayor when the city became operational on December 1, 2006. Already, he has shown progressive leadership in moving the city forward, as acknowledged in a recent award by the US conference of Mayors. With regard to the success of Johns Creek and the Public/Private partnership, Mayor Bodker had these comments:

> *After the residents of Johns Creek overwhelming vote in favor of incorporation, the community was faced with the obvious dilemma. How do you start up a city from scratch, almost literally overnight?*
>
> *In the final analysis, the Johns Creek Governor's Commission looked to our sister city to the south, Sandy Springs, and determined the public-private partnership model could potentially offer our citizens the best start-up. When our City Council was sworn in on November 14, 2006 the Commission recommended we use CH2M Hill OMI, the vendor that had been in place managing municipal services for the new city of Sandy Springs for one year.*
>
> *I do not believe we would have been able to achieve all that we did in our first year without following the public-private partnership model. The daunting task of standing up a city of 65,000 residents and first-year budget of $31.7 million – hiring employees, acquiring*

all the necessary equipment and systems, finding sufficient operating space and all the other administrative tasks – might have otherwise proved impossible.

Although it is a private entity, CH2M Hill OMI, has significant public sector experience and has been able use it to recruit professionals in their respective fields who now make up the majority of City Hall employees. I would say our Council has been very impressed with the high level of expertise and professionalism the partnership has brought to our management staff.

Satisfaction with hiring and human resource management is a key component of the model, as our City Manager has no direct hiring or firing authority over the staff he is charged with supervising. Thus far, because both partners have been successful in keeping healthy lines of communications open, it has not presented any insurmountable challenges. While we have no right to hire or fire outsourced employees, if we are dissatisfied with an individual's performance, the company takes steps to address the matter.

The citizens of Johns Creek also derive an "economy of scale" benefit through our partnership. Because the company has several municipal clients in close proximity to each other, we are able to share certain services. This allowed for almost immediate start-up on several fronts that may have otherwise began on a slower schedule in the traditional model. For example, our Geographic Information Systems (GIS) group was up and running almost immediately, as we were able to share that service with Sandy Springs and Milton, the third north Fulton City currently using this model. Our 24-hour call center, which allows us to keep the lines of communication open with our residents at all times also lent itself to this model. At the same time, since the model has the discipline of being driven by client satisfaction in line with profit margins, the incentive to keep costs low enters into the equation. This, and the high performance level of our professional staff, gives Johns Creek the distinction of having one of the lowest number of paid employees per capita in the state. That allows us to deliver on our promise to the citizens of responsible stewardship of tax dollars.

This is not to say things have been entirely smooth. But we have found that by keeping the lines of communication open, we are able to reach satisfactory resolution of any issues that do arise. If we want additional services that are not specified in our contract, we execute a change order and pay the difference accordingly – although there have been a few cases where the private company has gone beyond the scope with no additional cost to the city.

A key to the success of this model is the relationship between our City Manager – one of a handful of true city employees – and the company's Project Director. From the City Manager's perspective, he has been quick to embrace this new approach to government. On the company's side, it is imperative the Project Director listen well to suggestions and concerns, and balances service to the client with his responsibilities to the employee-owned company.

One aspect both sides have struggled a bit with is developing an appropriate set of performance metrics. In this regard the public-private model is not so different from traditional governments that also try to determine the best basis for assessing performance. But because such an evaluation is important in negotiations with the company, it may be more critical in this model.

Overall, I would say our City Management and our elected officials are pleased with the results of this innovative approach to government operations and it is serving our citizens well. Although the startup model is in and of itself unique, I would certainly support the exploration of the model not only for startup but for established municipalities as well."

Mayor Bodker spoke of many advantages accruing to the city from cost sharing, innovation and synergies. An actual example of all these factors is the Geographic Information System (GIS) that has been introduced. The basic system is shared by all the new cities, reducing costs. Each city's data is segregated within the system, making it appear to the user as a stand-alone system. Unlike many traditional cities (which have different, and sometimes incompatible departmental systems) for each P/P/P city the GIS system is the common platform for all the various systems needed by the many departments or functions. Great inefficiencies occur in many cities when, for example, the Planning and Development systems do not interact seamlessly with the Public Works systems. In the Sandy Springs model the platform is uniform for all departments: Finance, Revenue,

Public Works, Fire and Police, et al. Different departments may have special needs that require specialized software and/or confidentiality; but all are based on the GIS, assuring compatibility.

C. COST SHARING

The author is not aware of any significant cost sharing programs between Traditional cities. Every city tends to be an island unto itself.

Cost sharing in Public/Private Partnership cities may occur in at least two ways:

* Intercity
* City/Industry

1. Intercity

In the new Georgia cities, there are substantial savings available through Intercity cost sharing. As the new cities adopted the Sandy Springs model, they also benefited from the company's experience in the methods, systems and a trained work force that were available to be adapted to local conditions and data. Experienced corporate management was available to start the cities and then move on as their work was completed. Sandy Springs had benefited from the same
start-up expertise. The ability to bring in assistance from around the world, on short notice, at no additional cost, is unheard of in Traditional cities. This advantage continues today in the Public/Private partnership cities and will be available to existing cities that convert in the future.

As the base of P/P/P cities grows the advantages available from intercity cost sharing will also grow.

Frankly, due to the fixed cost contract for the first two years of operations, Sandy Springs has not had the immediate cost benefit that has been included in the contracts with the three newer cities In the longer run, all cities should benefit equally. One criteria that existing cities may want to consider is the company's ability to offer shared services.

The reader's reaction may be "We are not in Georgia so the Intercity sharing option is not available to us". As Public/Private Partnerships develop in other states, there will obviously be more opportunity for intercity cost sharing.

In the short run, many opportunities already exist. Consider that many of a city's operations are not location specific. In almost every function, there are "backroom" operations such as record keeping, accounting, data processing, purchasing, Information Technology, etc., that can be managed remotely. A good example of the widespread application of remote operations is found in the fourth, and smallest, of the new Georgia cities. – Chattahoochee Hill Country (CHC). Although CHC is located 50 miles from Sandy Springs, the preponderance of its services/functions are provided remotely by CH2MHill, the company that serves Sandy Springs, from its central location in Sandy Springs. Given the limited revenue available to the small new city of CHC, operations without this cost sharing would have been nearly impossible.

Tom Reed was the community leader in establishing the new city of Chattahoochee Hill Country. The city is a predominately rural area with a relatively small population. The area has enormous growth potential, but currently receives less than $2 million in annual revenue. Tom and his team of volunteers met the challenges of creating a full service government that could operate on the currently limited income, and still be adaptable for future growth, through the Public/Private partnership model.

He states:

> *There is simply no way that we could have stood our city up without the help of a private partner who had already been through the process. Our situation is quite unique, in that our city is an entirely rural area (with absolutely no civil infrastructure) only 25 minutes from the Atlanta airport. With the opening of a new four-lane Parkway through the area, there was a real danger of typical uncontained suburban sprawl which the people that live in our area particularly wanted to avoid. Since the only way that we could truly gain control*

of our zoning was to become a city; that was the direction that we chose.

That said, there is simply no precedent for a city of over 33,000 acres (with a broad, if limited infrastructure) and less than 3000 inhabitants (and extremely limited tax revenue) becoming a city (especially one with a unique and visionary zoning plan to proactively and permanently protect 70-80% of that land,but disallows many of the typical revenue-generators). Our difficult situation was exacerbated by legislative constraints which only allowed a matter of months to effect the transition. One advantage that we did have was a strong history of community activism and participation – over 5% of the community (150 people) participated in the various committees that researched and pushed for city-hood, and then went about actually implementing it. Our broad community effort and high level of communication ensured a high level of support for the innovative solutions needed to create our 'city that isn't a city'.

Our community had been closely following the experience of Sandy Springs and the other cities on the northern side of Atlanta that had also recently formed.All of them had elected to start their cities with a public-private partnership arrangement. However in each of their cases, there was already a substantial infrastructure and revenue stream to be taken over to support it. While the shared services scenario was certainly saving each of the municipalities a great deal of money, the fact was that each probably had enough gravity on its own to support a traditional city structure with some internal and some contracted services. What's more, while the cities were in fact relatively large geographically, their population density was similar to other local cities - there were many local analogs that could be modeled. That said, it was obvious to the leaders in those cities that there were huge benefits (in flexibility, savings, and speed of startup) to the outside vendor/shared services model.

In the case of the new City of Chattahoochee Hill Country, there simply were no reasonable analogs for comparison. It became apparent to the various volunteer groups working the problem that it would be almost impossible to raise a traditional city - one in which each job has to be done by a particular city employee. They were simply far too many "half jobs" (and "one day a month" jobs) and far too little revenue to support that traditional structure. In addition, because of the nontraditional zoning standard that our city had adopted (one which encourages large and relatively dense new urban style development in a few nodes while protecting the rural character of the bulk of the land), we knew that we needed serious support on the zoning and code enforcement side, at a level of competency which the typical city of 3000 simply can't attain.

After reviewing the experience of the other new cities in our area, it became immediately apparent that the vendor the other cities had selected (CH2M Hill) certainly had the required skill sets. In addition, having just set up all of those services and three other new cities, CH2MHill had both recent experience and available excess capacity that we were able to take advantage of.

Our biggest concern became ensuring that the vendor agreed there was a business case to be made for doing that in the current 'low volume of activity/low revenue' environment of our prospective city. We realized that if all of our planning was conducted with the expectation of a private public partnership which then did not come to fruition, there would simply not be enough time left to implement any alternative plan. Given that our growth projections call for a population of between 60-100,000 within the next 20 to 30 years (and the fact that there are not that many new cities of 90,000 being formed right now), we appreciated that we were a good investment for a partner with a long-term strategic point of view. CH2MHill was obviously interested in a 'small town' model as the obvious growth area of their private/public field of practice. There are a lot more small cities that could bring in a private vendor without the disruption that such intervention might cause a much larger and more established city. We knew that we were attractive on a long-term basis, and hoped that our private partner would find this a beneficial growth model (to the point that they might suffer a slightly lower level of return in the short term). Thankfully, they agreed.

Once we had that long-term commitment from our vendor, it became much easier for our many community groups to focus on "local flavor" input into policy areas. We were able to utilize a high level of expertise from field-specific experts that the vendor made available to us on an as needed basis that were high above the 'pay grade' that we could not have possibly afforded our own. The vendor also provided the cash necessary to fund all of these activities in advance of any revenue from the city. (Keep in mind that all of the work of creating the city, from laying out procedures and practices, compiling codes, providing and organizing public safety, lining up physical plant and employees, happened BEFORE the city came into existence or had any revenues). The vendor had to front the funding for all of these activities to the extent that volunteers or pro-bono services could not cover them.

Keep in mind, too, that as a volunteer group, we had no real authority to bind our new city. CH2M Hill did all of this work without any guarantee that the city would actually hire them after the fact (although the reality is that it would have been nearly impossible logistically to change that course once it had started). For both parties, it has been a very successful relationship of mutual respect and trust.

In any case, there have been very few regrets about our path.We HAVE successfully become the newest city in Georgia, and in doing so have achieved a number of successes that even the other cities in Georgia have not been able to match. Just as an example, our own city fire department went into action on 'Day One', providing us a level of protection equivalent to what we had been getting from the county at a lower price, and with far better customer service.We actually have full-time personnel in our centrally located, 'functional/not fancy' city hall every day to take inquires and provide information (something which used to take at least 1-2 hours round trip).

Other services, from code enforcement to public works, zoning to HR, courts to communications, are brought in on an as needed basis from other local cities under the shared services model. These ensure that we get true experts in each respective area, but only pay for the amount of time we need those experts. Because of those shared services, we can benefit from big city functionality – like our 24/7 call center (which is actually located in another municipality 50 miles away) – at a price that we can afford.

And it's not just that we can provide the services, and that the services are better. Not only are we saving money by taking advantage of flexible staffing, but we also benefit from group purchasing, which helps everywhere from road repairs to toilet paper. Even more importantly, we avoid the typical small-town problem of just a few direct employees who are constantly inefficiently multi-tasking, working on every discipline, expert at none. Instead, we parachute true experts in, as needed, to deal with specific areas of expertise, secure in the knowledge that if they need backup, the vendor's deep bench assures its availability. We can swing far above the typical small city's weight as a result.

As a forgotten corner of the county, we had never had much in the way of 'customer service' from our county, and aside from some truly visionary help on our zoning plan, little in the way of official support. Our city organizing group's many volunteers made clear to their fellow citizens that, with our limited income, cityhood was not going to bring any bounty of new services. But we HAVE delivered on the promise that what little we could afford in the level of services would be responsive, friendly, and cost-effective. And we DO now have control over the land use and planning of our 33,000 unspoiled acres. Our newly elected officials can count on the deep bench of our partner, CH2MHill to do the heavy lifting while they focus on development, policies and priorities, and other constituency-related issues, secure in the knowledge that they have all of the tools that they need at their disposal.

While it is clear that Mr. Reed is speaking to the cost sharing benefits for starting a new city, these same benefits will be experienced in existing cities that enjoy a Public/Private partnership.

A specific example of a cost sharing function that has been of great benefit is the innovative Customer Response Center (CRC) or Call Center. Customer Response is the better name since the system does much more than answer calls. The primary reason for creating the new city was to offer a more responsive government. The CRC was designed to meet that specific requirement. The citizens were tired of automated responses to calls and the apparent ineffectiveness of government employees to respond to their needs on the rare occasion when an actual person could be reached.

The CRC features live answers to all calls – 24 hours a day, seven days a week. The attendants are trained to be able to respond to many of the needs, and have Frequently Asked Questions (FAQ) on their screens. When an immediate answer is not available, the attendants route the call to the appropriate department. The response does not end there. Simultaneously, if action is required, a work order is entered into the system which also is directed to the involved department(s).

A requirement of the contract is that a response must be given to the caller within 48 hours that the problem has been solved or when it will be done; (two hours if it is deemed an emergency, such as trees are being cut unlawfully)

In addition to the answer and response functions the CRC also provides for the collection of important data by creating a record of every call to allow the identification and reporting of trends in citizen needs and desires.

Our citizens have been astounded and pleased with this service, as indicated by their responses. The volume of calls handled in 2007 was over 200,000 as citizens have come to know that they are able to receive good and prompt responses.

There are few, if any, municipal governments that answer every call with a live voice on a 24 hour basis without the use of queues or interactive voice response technology. The reader may question how a live response system can be cost effective in this age when almost all governments and businesses have gone to automated response systems (or NON response systems as some have characterized them). The answer is both innovation and cost sharing.

The CRC designed for the P/P/P cities shares the cost between the cities. Callers do not realize that they have reached a shared facility because there are separate groups of responders assigned to each city with different FAQ lists and different referral routes. However, in peak volume times the responder groups are crossed trained to help each other. In addition, in even more severe peaks, the calls are automatically referred to an answering service that takes the live call and makes the necessary referral. All indications are that the public is pleased with the handling of peak calls.

These innovative and sharing procedures have kept the costs to a minimum while providing the public with service that in these times is considered to be "gold plated".

Another innovative example of cost sharing is the "cross swearing" of code enforcement officers. Enforcement of building and zoning codes had been very lax in the previously unincorporated areas in which the new cities were formed. Therefore, there was a need to greatly increase the personnel involved with enforcement of the codes. In Georgia, code enforcement officers are sworn in much like police officers. The ability to cross swear officers so that they may serve in more than one city allows a very efficient use of their valuable time.

There are many other examples large and small of cost sharing, but collectively these efforts contribute substantially to the financial condition of the cities and to the citizens' satisfaction.

Functions that lend themselves to cost sharing and centralization include most of the core administration: Human Resources, IT, accounting, finance, zoning and permitting, record keeping for police and fire, to cite a few.

2. City/Industry

In the previous section, we already discussed some of the value to Public/Private partnerships of sharing equipment and personnel with other cities.

Now consider that a further sharing is taking place. There is a sharing of resources between the cities and industry. This occurs when a P/P/P company has business, such as paving or maintenance, with other industry ventures. The company may, in a given period, need the resource for a few days each week in the city. For the remaining time, the resource may be redirected to meet the other industry needs. Maximum utilization of the equipment takes place, with savings to the city. Information Technology is an example of an area that lends itself to resource sharing of this type, and is also an area where major capital expenditures or leases may be avoided.

D. FLEXIBILITY

The Public/Private Partnership model offers superior flexibility in the utilization of both people and materials.

Let us first examine the experience with personnel. Flexibility has occurred in several ways;

1. As previously mentioned, there seems to be a greater ability to move personnel from department to department.

2. Short term needs are met by temporary interdepartmental movement, by bringing in temporary resources from other areas of the company, or by short term contracts. Under the Sandy Springs model, neither of these methods has caused additional cost to the city because they have been covered under the fixed cost service contract.

A good example of this flexibility occurred in the early months of city-hood. The county transferred around 800 incomplete building permits to the new city. These were permits for which the county had collected fees, but had been sitting on for several months. Since the city planners had anticipated a stream of about 50 permits per month, this backlog was a major problem. The company (CH2MHill) responded by bringing in the necessary people to clear the backlog – and then they were gone. It was a very quick and efficient response that did not burden the city with a long-term personnel commitment.

E. REDUCED LIABILITIES

1. Personnel

A major, and growing, concern of government at all levels, is the issue of long term liabilities for pensions and benefits. State and local governments have more than $1 trillion in unfunded liabilities for pensions and retirement medical benefits. Many local governments have recognized the problem and are seeking solutions. Others still appear to be unaware of the growing problem; or if they do recognize the problem, have no idea what to do about it. Attempts to curtail benefits, or to shift from defined benefits to defined contribution plans, often meet with considerable opposition from employees and unions.

An example of a large city that has fallen victim to major financial liabilities is San Diego. It may amaze most people to learn that such a vibrant city, with so many positive attributes, could be in financial difficulty. Yet, due to unfunded liabilities for pensions and benefits of over a billion dollars, the city was in dire financial straits.

The new mayor has recognized that innovative steps are needed to help the city recover from the hole that it is in. The author was asked to speak to a conference organized by the mayor. The purpose was to kick off a campaign to gain approval for a referendum to allow consideration of the use of private industry to become legal in San Diego. The referendum passed. Time will tell whether a Public/Private partnership can be initiated over the objection of their strong unions and the effect of political inertia. The point of relating this situation is to illustrate that even fine cities can fall victim to overwhelming liabilities for pensions and benefits.

One of the most significant values of the P/P/P model is that it minimizes a government's potential financial liabilities.

In the Sandy Springs model, there are no long term liabilities associated with personnel, except for public safety functions which are not a part of the P/P/P. All core personnel liabilities are the responsibility of the private company. For small to medium sized cities, in addition to avoiding the liabilities, not having to manage and fund the retirement and benefit programs is of substantial value.

2. Capital Investments

In the same manner that personnel liabilities can drain a city's coffers, the requirement for longer term investments in major equipment and systems can be a significant cost item. An example is heavy road equipment, either for maintenance or construction. Many existing cities find it necessary to own capital intensive equipment that is not only expensive to maintain, but also frequently idle. A costly city garage may be required to repair, maintain and house such equipment.

In the Public/Private Partnership model, the city does not own or maintain equipment. No depreciation, no maintenance costs, no maintenance facilities, and no management resources are required of the city. The savings are substantial.

F. RISKS

The following chart is a simplified illustration of the risks normally experienced by the pubic sector that can be shifted to or shared by a private partner. The very substantial risks to the city for the long term liability for personnel pensions and benefits, and asset ownership and maintenance have been discussed previously.

Risk Allocation in Public-Private Partnerships			
Risk	**Responsibility**		
	Private Partner	**Public Partner**	**Shared**
Meeting all service expectations	X		
* Financing and accounting	X		
* Community development	X		
* Public Works	X		
Human resource administration	X		
Public Safety			
* Police		X	
* Fire		X	
Emergency 911		X	
Meeting contractual obligations	X		
Customer responsiveness	X		
Public input/involvement			X
Non-performance	X		
Budget authorization/allocation		X	
Costs in excess of budget	X		
Non-compliance with environmental regulations	X		
Asset management	X		
Asset repair and replacement	X		
Indemnification			X
Insurance			X

G. TAXATION

One of the myths expounded by opponents to the creation of the cities was that taxes would go up. Let the record show that in all four new cities there was **no increase** in the property tax rate or any other tax rates. The cities have experienced substantial growth which has resulted in increased revenues. With this growth and prudent management, Sandy Springs, by it second year of operation, has not only been able to avoid increasing tax rates, but has succeeded in building an $18 million reserve (approximately20% of the annual budget).

Existing cities that convert to the Sandy Springs model should experience similar results. With the increased efficiency offered by the model, cities will have the choice of **(1) decreasing taxes, (2) retiring debt, (3) increasing reserves or (4) improving services**. All of the foregoing are worthwhile goals, and all are rare attainments in the current environment of Traditional cities.

CHAPTER III

What is the structure of government that will best guard against the precipitate counsels and factious combinations for unjust purposes...
-James Madison

STRUCTURE

A common misconception about the Sandy Springs model is that "the company runs the city". Nothing could me further from the truth. The following is the basic structure and a simple chain of command for the model.

ELECTED OFFICIALS
*
CITY MANAGER
*
PRIVATE COMPANY

A. ELECTED OFFICIALS

The elected officials (Mayor and Council) set the policies for the city. They pass the ordinances, set priorities, approve/disapprove zoning and permitting, adopt long range plans, set the budget, and handle all policy issues.

B. CITY MANAGER

The City Manager is an experienced professional in city administration. It is his responsibility to assure the council's policies are carried out and that the day-to-day work of the city is accomplished. To fulfill this function, he is in direct supervision of the private company.

C. PRIVATE COMPANY

The private company performs the work as directed by the City Manager.

So long as each of the three tiers focuses on the assigned role, the city will, and does, perform effectively. In this requirement for role adherence, the Public/Private Partnership cities are no different than Traditional cities.

Under this chain of command, a typical P/P/P city structure might be as follows:

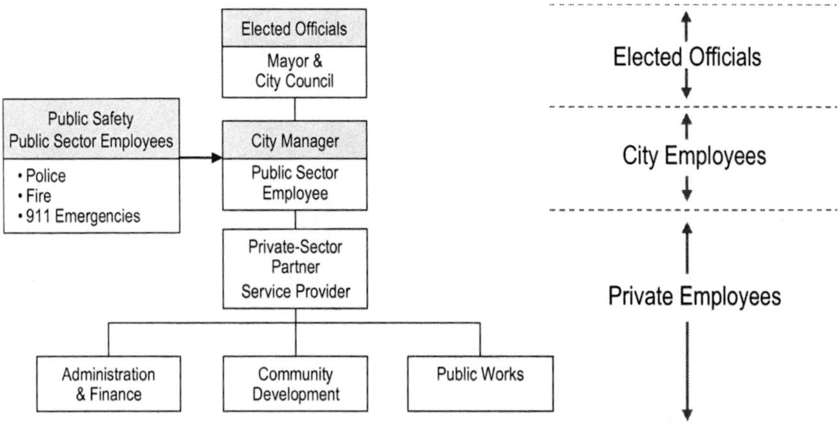

Public-Private Partnership Model – Total Outsourcing

An important example of the hierarchical structure in action might be the preparation of the budget. As in a Traditional city, the functional units of the company compile preliminary data outlining the costs to carry out the anticipated programs of the council. The data is received by the City Manager. He is assisted in matching revenues to expenses to prepare a draft budget. The resulting draft is presented by the City Manager to the Council for approval or amendment.

This is a gross simplification of the complex task of arriving at a budget, but serves to illustrate the designated roles.

It should be clear that the company does not "run the city".

D. CITY MANAGER CHARACTERISTICS

At this point, we need to focus on the important role of the city Manager, and the characteristics required in carrying out that role in a Public/ Private partnership.

The City Manager is the chief operating officer. As such, he has sole responsibility for carrying out the policies and providing the services mandated by the elected officials.

The experience requirements of a City Manager in a Traditional city and in a P/P/P may be similar. The personal characteristics that are required to succeed may be quite different.

Many city managers will have the ability and desire to be a good P/P/P manager. In many ways, the P/P/P job may be easier. A prime factor is that the P/P/P manager has far fewer personnel issues to manage. Anyone in either a government or industry supervisory position knows that much of a manager's time is tied up with personnel matters. With a reduction in personnel matters, the city Manager will have more time to focus on the big picture.

In the same manner, the budgeting process is simplified for the City Manager. A large portion of the budget is predetermined by the P/P/P contract.

The City Manager will also have access to invaluable outside resources. All the above and more, make the job much more rewarding.

Does this mean that any City Manager is suited to lead a P/P/P? No, there are some important characteristics that a P/P/P manager should possess. First, the Manager must be open to change, creativity and innovation. The P/P/P represents a totally new approach to getting the job done. After a career in the Traditional model, many City Managers will not wish to, or be able to adapt. Others will relish the opportunity to effect positive change.

Second, the "new" city manager becomes more of an executive, setting the direction, while leaving it to the company to carry out the directives. One should not infer that the City Manager does not have the ability to delve into any operation to whatever depth is needed. Rather, the fact is that the need to do hands-on management is diminished.

The individual who may best be able to reflect the effectiveness of the Sandy Springs model of Public/Private partnership is the City Manager, John McDonough. After an exhaustive nationwide search for a manager with experience in city government and also the personal characteristics that would enable him to adjust to a radically new model for providing services to the new city, John McDonough was selected. His performance has lived up to the community's high expectations as he has helped to evolve this partnership model.

John offered the following assessment of the model from the viewpoint of the man right in the middle of it all.

> *Eight o'clock a.m. on December first two-thousand and five marked a bold new beginning for Sandy Springs, Georgia when it opened its doors for the first time and began providing all general government municipal services through a contract with a private sector engineering firm. After a thirty year struggle for self-determination this suburban community of almost 90,000 residents had become a city. The leaders of this movement to become an independent city determined early on that the status quo, characterized by high costs and poor services, was no way to run a government. They shifted their sights to how to best utilize non-traditional methods to build a model government operation for the Twenty-first Century. Their*

vision was to establish an accountable and responsive government built on the concept of customer service, efficiency, innovation and value.

The election of a group of forward thinking City Councilmember's made this vision a reality. One of the first matters for consideration by the new City Council was a vote to outsource most of its services. In what was to be the largest outsourcing of local government services in United States history, the Sandy Springs City Council approved a twenty-nine million dollar first year contract with CH2M Hill OMI to provide all general government services including: Planning, zoning, public works, streets, facilities, information technology, human resources, administrative support, revenue collection, financial management services, procurement, purchasing, communications, transportation planning, capital project planning and management, parks and recreation, code enforcement, plans review, permitting and municipal court services.

Sandy Springs operates under the Council-Manager form of government where the Mayor and Council set policy and make the laws governing the City. The City Manager is appointed by the Mayor and Council and is responsible for the day-to-day operation of all government services including: police, fire, emergency management and general government functions. In the case of Sandy Springs the City Manager is responsible to the Council for overseeing the contract with CH2M Hill for the provision of general government services.

Highlights of Outsourcing Model

The Sandy Springs service delivery model is built on the premise that the government will provide a superior level of customer service in all areas. In order to accomplish this goal the City, through its contract with CH2M Hill, established a twenty-four hour a day, seven day a week Citizen Response Center (CRC) where trained customer responders answer calls. No calls are answered by an automated voice system. The CRC serves as the first point of contact for most citizen and business inquiries. The CRC processes calls and routes requests for service to the appropriate department for action. Once the customer request has been completed a return call is made to let the customer know the matter has been resolved. For the last twelve months the CRC processed more than 160,000 total calls.

The Sandy Springs contract for services and the relationship it has with its private sector partner has several unique features that help to set it apart from traditional governments. Those features include:

1. *Reach back assistance to corporate headquarters for specialized expertise that is not typically resident at a local government;*

2. *Significant flexibility in reallocating resources within the contract;*

3. *Regularly scheduled replacement of operating equipment; and*

4. *Prompt mitigation of any personnel deficiencies.*

Reach Back Assistance
Operating governments at all levels has become increasingly challenging and many communities find that they do not have the resident expertise on staff to address complex issues. Because of our contract with CH2M Hill, an international engineering services company with over 23,000 employees, the City of Sandy Springs has access to a broad range of professionals to assist us with finding innovative solutions to difficult issues. We are able to request technical assistance on a broad range of topics such as meeting federal storm water requirements, analyzing municipal water systems, evaluating software records systems for police, fire and emergency medical services, and finding ways to create sustainable communities.

Flexibility in Reallocating Resources

Demands on municipal service departments can change for any number of different reasons. Due to budgetary constraints, bureaucratic rules and entrenched civil service systems, traditional governments have little flexibility in reallocating resources to respond to changes in demand. The outsourcing model in Sandy Springs allows for the expeditious shifting of resources when the need arises allowing us to respond quickly to changes in customer service requests. We are often able to shift resources (equipment, services and personnel) from one service area to another without changing the overall terms of the contract. However, if we exceed the resources available in the contract we would then have to agree on a change in scope of services and negotiate an appropriate fee for additional services rendered.

Scheduled Replacement of Operating Equipment

The right technology can be a powerful service multiplier in today's workplace. However, due to the rapid development of new and improved applications and the equipment needed to support them, the average useful life for software and hardware is just a few years. Recognizing that these tools are perishable items that must be updated regularly in order to remain relative, our contract calls for industry leading technology replenishment on a 36 month basis. This schedule allows for adequate lead time to evaluate, test, procure, install and utilize these necessary tools. The great benefit to the City is that it can avoid the significant upfront costs associated with having to purchase and replace traditional IT systems.

Prompt Mitigation of Personnel Deficiencies

At one time or another every organization experiences personnel challenges that impact its ability to effectively perform its mission. In most traditional governments it often takes months or even years to make changes in personnel assignments due to civil service systems and other personnel rules that make it very difficult to replace non-performing employees. Under the Sandy Springs outsourcing model, general government employees are on the CH2M Hill payroll and providing service to the City of Sandy Springs. If there is an instance where an employee is not meeting expectations, the private company may take immediate action to make a change in personnel. In an instance where the City Manager believes a change needs to be made the contract allows the manager to ask for an immediate replacement or reassignment of an employee. Under the outsourcing model the private sector has incentives to perform and to ensure prompt action when personnel issues arise.

Summary

Over the past two years, the Sandy Springs experiment has shown that outsourcing general government services to the private sector can work extremely well. All indications are that citizens are very pleased with the improved level of service, and the value they are receiving for services provided. Our citizen customers continue to comment that they like to be able to contact a live person to discuss their issues twenty-four hours a day and appreciate the fact that they will receive a prompt response to their inquiries. At a time when the resources available at all levels of government are becoming increasingly difficult to come by, communities are faced with a stark choice: to continue business as usual by cutting services and raising taxes, or look to the efficiencies of the private sector as a viable option to provide essential services to our communities. All one needs to do is visit Sandy Springs to see that the vision that the City's founders established for an accountable and responsive government, is alive and doing extremely well.

CHAPTER IV

IN CONTRACTS, THE PARTIES DETERMINE, AT LEAST IN PART, WHAT THEIR OBLIGATION ONE TO ANOTHER WILL BE - The Columbia Encyclopedia

CONTRACTS

A. SEEEKING A CONTRACT

Once the decision is made to consider a Public/Private partnership, there are many avenues available to obtain a contract. State laws may determine the process in some states.

Absent specific legal constraints, a city may choose to:

1. Enter into competitive bidding by issuing a Request for Proposal (RFP). A sample RFP is provided in Attachment B. Every city will have unique needs that are expounded within the elements of the proposal, but this document will provide a proven format and suggest many of the functions to be considered.

2. Engage in a sole source negotiation with a single firm. If this course is chosen, it is suggested that the process begin with a Request for Qualifications (RFQ) or a Request for information (RFI) to assure that the firm has the necessary ability to meet the

city's needs. The RFP in Attachment B will also be a useful guide in recognizing the elements to be addressed in an RFQ/I.

B. FORM OF CONTRACT

It is obvious that the form and terms of the contract are critical in a Public/Private partnership. The author recommends that the city should place as many core functions/services as possible within the contract, to take advantage of the synergies and efficiencies offered. Therefore, the contract assumes major importance.

Conventional wisdom is that contracts must be as detailed as possible; that every function should be covered by very specific measurements. Our experience is that conventional wisdom is wrong.

In the months that preceded the new city of Sandy Springs, the author, in his voluntary role of Interim City Manager, received advice from many sources that was in line with conventional thought. While listening carefully to all this well meant advice, we decided to adopt a different approach. We knew that the key to a successful contract was to focus on "partnership" As discussed in other sections; the contract was structured to be inclusive of the largest feasible range of functions/services. There was also a conscious decision to allow as much opportunity as possible for the company to be innovative and to allow the maximum flexibility in utilizing resources. A contract of this nature requires a significant level of trust between the parties (for a specific example of successful contracts, the reader may wish to refer to the author's book, *Creating the New City of Sandy Springs*; Appendix C of that book offers a sample contract. By contrast, conventional contracts attempt to eliminate any trace of trust by over-specifying and over-measuring.

The result of employing a less rigid contract has paid great dividends to the Public/Private partnership cities that have followed the Sandy Springs model. The company (CH2MHill) has exceeded expectations in every area. Not only have financial targets been met, but of most importance, responsiveness to the public has also exceeded expectations, and far outstripped the performance of Traditional cities in Georgia.

Throughout the book, we have referred to the "private" partner in a P/P/P as a single entity; one company that provides all the services under the agreement. It actuality, there is no such company. The private partner is the manager of a number of other partners or sub-contractors. However, it is essential to the city that its partner – the managing partner - be the single point of contract and be totally responsible for all the services that it manages.

The chain of command, from the elected officials through the City Manager to the managing partner, must be unbroken. For the optimum results to occur, the managing partner must be the single point of contact to provide the benefits of efficiency, synergy, cost sharing and other factors that have been discussed throughout this book.

To the city, the managing partner is the only visible entity. To the public the only visible entity is the city. All the various sub contractors, each of whom play a vital role in the provision of services, do so in relative obscurity. Effectively, they are seen collectively as "city employees".

To provide an example of the many firms that work cohesively under the direction of the managing partner, let us examine the new Public/ Private partnerships in Georgia. The private partner company has made a major financial commitment to serving local governments through public/private partnerships. The company has shown a complete understanding of the role of the managing partner as the integrator of a number of service providers. As the principal, the managing partner, under the contract may choose to provide the service directly by use of its own personnel and assets, or by sub-contracting the functions. To the city the choice is not material. The company is seen as the provider. The buck stops there.

The ability of the managing partner to coordinate all the cities' services providers into a seamless operation is vital.

As Public/Private partnership opportunities expand to existing cities, the managing partner's ability to negotiate even more advantageous contracts with sub-contractors should be enhanced. Subs will take notice of the expanding market and recognize the opportunity to enjoy the benefits accruing from the economy of scale. They will be encouraged to price services, and perform, at levels that will insure a presence on the team.

The agreements with sub-contractors provide a mechanism to make changes if any service is not considered to be satisfactory. These agreements tend to be for a period that is shorter than the Public/Private partnership, and contain very specific service criteria. Such criteria are possible because the functions being performed by each Sub are fairly narrow in scope. If a sub does not perform up to the standard, the managing partner can terminate the contract and engage a substitute company. Such a change, although rare to date, is largely unnoticed by the public.

The author has described an interlocking system of companies that may seem more complex than it actually is in practice. The fact is, the model works extremely well in the cities that have adopted it.

Skeptics will, no doubt, always continue to expect the P/P/P relationship to sour. It may, but it should not happen. If city officials restrain themselves from attempting to micromanage the process, the private company will continue to exceed expectations. The company will be driven to perform by self interest.

First, the contracts offer the firm an opportunity to make a healthy profit. Beyond the profitability, the company has demonstrably enjoyed the opportunity to be creative; to work with the "clean sheet of paper" in bringing improved methodology.

Second, this Public/Private partnership opportunity has the potential to open a huge new market for industry. The author has estimated that if all the traditional cities were to convert to P/P/P's, the market available to private industry could approximate $90 Billion.

A final reason why the contract (as introduced in the Sandy Springs model) has limited risk to the city is that the city has recourse if it is dissatisfied with the company's performance. In the P/P/P contracts for the new cities there is a provision that allows the contract to be terminated without cause. In addition there are provisions for making the transition work, should it be necessary to terminate.

The "terminate without cause" provision is the ultimate hammer! Naturally, it should be executed only as the last resort; but, it provides important insurance to the city.

1. TERM OF CONTRACT

Initially, a multiyear contract is desirable for both partners. There must be time for the new methodology to be implemented and tested. Companies will be loath to invest the resources necessary to set up the city, and to provide first rate services, if there is no reasonable expectation of a long term relationship. In Georgia, however, such contracts must be for no more than one year. Therefore, in Sandy Springs, the contract is for six years, with a clause requiring annual renewal. This clause gives both parties an opportunity to evaluate the success of the partnership on a yearly basis and to make adjustments to the contract as warranted.

2. PAYMENT TERMS

Options for the type of contractual payments that may occur in any public/Private partnership include:
Cost plus fixed fee - this type contract is low risk for the contractor and typically carries a higher cost escalation risk for the city.

Time and materials - This type of contract also contains more risk for the city but traditionally uses an open-book accounting methodology. It may have an upper limit or "not to exceed" amount. This method carries with it a high administrative cost because of the detailed accounting and reporting.

Lump sum or Fixed Price – This may be the most desirable type of contract to the city because it provides more certainty about the costs for running the operations while providing the contractor with an incentive to increase profit margins through technologies and efficiencies.

The contracts for the new Georgia Public/Private partnership cities all provide for fixed price payments to the company. The options to employ cost-plus, or time and material, payment methods were available, but there were several factors that influenced the decision to adopt the fixed cost method.

Factors considered important in this decision included:

(1) the desire to avoid financial surprises. The cities had good revenue projections, and the fixed costs that were proposed could be funded.

(2) the desire to allow the company maximum flexibility in meeting service needs.

With the annual renewal clause, the partners have the capability of renegotiating the payment method should it be desirable in the future.

3. REVENUES

It may be important to some to note that under the contract, the company does not touch the city's revenues. All revenues from taxes, fees, and other sources, flow directly to the city. Under the fixed cost contract, the company receives a monthly check that represents one-twelfth of the annual contract amount. This allows protection of funds, minimization of cost accounting, and simplification of budgeting for both the city and the company.

4. PERFORMANCE MEASUREMENTS

Performance measurements can be a two-edged sword. Properly constructed, measurements and standards may provide the city with an understanding of the level of performance in providing the required services. However, poorly focused measurements can result in less than optimal performance.

Service providers will direct their employees and resources at meeting the measurement. In doing this, other worthwhile services may be given less attention. If the standard is not high enough, performance will be sub-optimal and the desired levels of service may not be met.

If the bar is set too high, the service provider and its employees will be discouraged and may fail to perform.

Given these potential problems, much attention is often focused on identifying and quantifying performance metrics. A commonly held opinion with regard to performance measurements is that the more metrics that can be created, with more details, the better. Maybe that opinion holds true for Traditional governments. If the management and employees seem to have little incentive to perform, the need for setting minimum standards and measuring performance against those standards has some merit.

The approach to performance measurements that has allowed P/P/P's to excel has been an important difference in attitude. Rather than the city imposing unilateral standards and metrics which could be used to impose service levels, under the P/P/P model the process has been a joint effort. Metrics are most valuable when both partners agree and support the definition of the service to be measured and the optimal level of performance.

For this reason, it has been preferable to not overemphasize metrics in the original contract. The city and the corporation need at least a year of operations to properly design a usable set of metrics whose emphasis is placed on correct areas, and which does not inhibit the company in innovating and the flexible use of resources.

Every city has a different set of needs and priorities. The establishment of performance measurements to assist in meeting those needs should be approached in a reasoned manner and in a spirit of cooperation.

CHAPTER V

It is very rare that you meet obstacles in this world that the humblest man has not the facilities to urmount - Henry David Thoreau

OBSTACLES

The progressive leader who chooses to pursue the consideration of the Public/Private partnership model for an existing city must be prepared to face a number of obstacles. Chief among the hurdles will be both legal and political objections. Before losing heart, such leaders should read my list of "there is no way's" in Chapter VI. Many will tell you that something cannot be done. Only a select few leaders can make difficult things happen. However, we should take a realistic look at the types of obstacles that may present themselves.

A. LEGAL

Step one in the process of converting a city to a Public/Private partnership is to assess the laws governing the city. Every state, and every city, may operate under a different set of statutes. Some may have prohibitions against a city contracting for services. For example, San Diego, which was addressed earlier, had such a statute. It was necessary to change the statute by a referendum.

In other cases there may be various forms of restrictions on how contracts may be let. For example, there may be laws that limit the term of contracts, or specify bidding procedures, or require the selection of the low bidder, etc. It is important to understand any restrictions in advance so that a path may be found to allow the process to proceed. If there is no way to work within the restrictions, remember that laws can be changed. Having to seek changes may slow the progress, but it will not stop it.

B. POLITICAL

Once the legal processes for conversion are understood, the next barrier to conversion is likely to rear up in the political arena. There will be many individuals and organizations that have a vested interest in maintaining the status quo. Unfortunately, most of the opposition will be placing their own personal interests ahead of the citizens'.

Individuals in opposition may range from existing city employees whose concerns are quite reasonable, to those who simply have an unreasonable knee jerk reaction to the concept.

With regard to employees, the better performers will be very likely to be offered jobs, while the less productive will not.

Often the people who exhibit knee jerk reactions are the most troublesome, because their concerns are not founded on a factual basis. Many times, we have found that great concerns have been raised and widely circulated on the basis of pure fabrication and ignorance.

The author attended a meeting in one community, where written material was circulated stating explicitly that taxes on senior citizens had been raised by seventy percent in Sandy Springs. Naturally, the senior citizens in the community were immediately upset and opposed to the cityhood proposal. In truth, there had been no increase in the millage rate for seniors (or any other taxpayers) in Sandy Springs. Furthermore, the Sandy Springs Council is prohibited, by law, from imposing any increase without a referendum of the citizens.

Unfounded concerns are difficult to erase because they are emotional. Often as soon as a concern is revealed to be of dubious validity, it will pop up again in a different form, or place, and the confrontation begins all over again. *C'est la guerre.*

Organizations in opposition may include: firms that currently hold contracts with the city, unions, the media (who seem to often oppose private industry as a matter of practice), and any group that feels that it has an "in" with the current city administration.

An example of the last group might be developers. Such organizations may present a difficult barrier. They can be capable and well funded to mount a public relations campaign against the conversion. They may also wield considerable influence with elected officials. The best defense against such attacks may be a good offense. The community should be made aware of the self interest of such groups and constantly reminded that there is a more efficient and responsive model available to the city.

There is a tendency to be overly concerned with attacks by the opposition. One's normal reaction is to immediately fire off a rebuttal to any statement. Experience has shown that it is better to wait until the leadership has a firm understanding of the plan for conversion before going public. Do not become trapped into squabbling over issues that have no basis in reality.

CHAPTER VI

The future is a world limited by ourselves
- Maurice Maeterlinck

FUTURE

Even though the citizens of the new Public/Private partnership cities can testify to the benefits of the Sandy Springs model as opposed to the previously provided county services, there is still the legitimate question as to whether the P/P/P model will perform better than Traditional governments in existing cities. All indications are that it will.

A. COMPARATIVE CITIES STUDY

To provide a definitive answer to the question, the respected research facilities of the Georgia Institute of Technology (Georgia Tech) have been enlisted to conduct a study. The outline of the study is provided in Appendix A

The author has been designated as a Research Fellow to assist in formulating the study methodology. The study will examine the performance of Public/Private partnership cities versus comparable Traditional cities. The comparison will include:

(1) financial performance and,

(2) citizens' satisfaction

James D. White, Ph.D. at Georgia Tech's Center for Advanced Communications Technology (CACP) addressed the study as follows;

> *The CACP in partnership with the Reason Foundation is conducting an evaluative study to develop a clear picture of the relative merits and pitfalls of the concept in general, and associated "best practices," including questions of use of technology, of communication, and of political participation. The multicity case study approach will explore five cases of outsourcing implementation in comparison to five comparative "Traditional" control along the dimensions of budgets, efficacy of service delivery and citizen perception using baseline evaluations, survey and interview methodologies.*
>
> *The study's key research question focuses on a comparative study of contract and traditional cities, with respect to the implementation of municipal service outsourcing, and how these lessons may be applied to local government. The aim is to develop optimal approaches to efficient, efficacious, and socially beneficial governance."*

It is anticipated that the study will be completed by the third quarter of 2008. Until then, there is ample evidence, both data and anecdotal, that the P/P/P model is providing superior financial and service benefits. For example, we know that Sandy Springs' costs are substantially lower (approximately 20%) than were forecast for running a Traditional city. The city has had two years of successful performance while living well within the budget. Given that the time for setting up the city was only a few months, the high level of initial performance is rather incredible. The author can only attribute that performance to the Public/Private partnership.

B. EXISTING CITY CONVERSIONS

We know that Public/Private partnerships are the best structures for establishing new cities. The choice of four recently incorporated cities to use this model and the success of these cities is good evidence in favor of the model. While the advantages that industry brought to the table were vital to setting up the new cities; those attributes have also been important in sustaining the superior performance. Those sustainable factors can, (and, in the opinion of the author, should) be transferable to existing cities.

Rather than questioning whether there are benefits to be gained by conversion of cities to the new model, city leaders should be asking the question, "Why not"? Why indeed, if there is a model that appears to offer such promise, are we not willing, at the very least, to consider a change? The answers probably are bound up in several bundles. Among those are: simple inertia, lack of a strong leader, fear of trying new things, union opposition, employee fears, and just plain old politics. If one is in office and no one is threatening to evict, why risk a change? The answer to the last question should be, "because the citizens will be better served".

Many existing cities have begun to examine their options. The author has been involved with several.

Two cities that have taken recent steps to implement the Public/Private partnership model are Central, Louisiana and Bonita Springs, Florida. At the time of this writing, Central is in the process of negotiating a P/P/P contract. Bonita Springs has issued a Request for Proposal (RFP) for a company to take over the city's community development services, a core administrative function.

Across the country, the widespread introduction of full Public/private partnerships has not yet occurred. However, there are a great number of examples of outsourcing of specific services and privatization.

Dr. Adrian Moore, Vice President of the Reason Foundation has observed:

> *"In recent decades various forms of outsourcing of local government services has been widespread in the U.S.*
>
> - *According to the latest survey by the International City/County Management Association, on average local governments outsource to private firms about 20% of services.*

- *Motivations for outsourcing range from access to new skills, flexibility, improving quality and saving money.*

- *Cost savings are often the most important motive. Savings range from 5% to 60% depending on the service in question and how much change outsourcing brings. Typical cost savings are 10-15%.*

- *Local government outsourcing has become richer with experience, with more performance based contracting and better management and oversight systems."*

Other cities should be taking similar initiatives over the next several years. Particularly in states where the economy, or changes in tax structures, have placed pressure on the finances of local governments. It is unfortunate that crises have to be the main driver of positive change, but such is often the case in our political arenas.

What will it take to jump start local leaders to consider alternative methods for serving the cities for which they are responsible? Two elements are needed: One is a "hero"; a leader who is willing to risk his political neck to provide the citizens a better city. The second is good data that will provide the hero with a basis for supporting change. We are working on securing the data.

The study currently underway at Georgia Tech should provide both financial and citizen satisfaction data that is both objective and comprehensive. In the short run, a vigorous examination of the success of the new Public/Private partnership cities should be enough to convince any unbiased city official that the model is worth pursuing. Earlier, an estimate of the potential market for private industry, if all local governments were to convert to the Sandy Springs model, was provided at the $90 billion level. Based on the recent experience with the Public/Private partnership cities, the American public could experience a $20 billion savings if such a conversion should take place.

While it is unreasonable to expect a total conversion to the Public/Private partnership model in my lifetime, there is time to begin substantial movement toward more effective local government.

Let us consider some of the services that may be considered for conversion to a Public/Private partnership.

ADMINISTRATIVE SERVICES

Accounting and Financial

Capital Program administration
Forecasting and policy implementation
Contract administration
Communications and Public Relations
Purchasing
Payroll
Human Relations functions
Benefits administration

Departmental support

Overall administrative support to all service functions and departments
Administration of Emergency Preparedness Plans

Information Technology and Web Site

Centralized management of all network resources
Centralized storage of records
Data security and backup
Software and hardware uniformity
Archive data and emails
Data base for occupational and business licenses
Access all data 24/7
Web site hosting, design and maintenance
Develop, update, maintain and service GIS data
Include utilities and infrastructure in GIS Service
Make GIS data available to public and contractors

Records Management Program

Implement and maintain document management System
Maintain system to preserve document security
Protect document integrity
Provide application server to store and manage data
Provide and maintain access to data
Design storage strategies and systems
Implement and coordinate transfer of data as necessary

COMMUNITY DEVELOPMENT SERVICES

Planning and Zoning

Provide information to public
Provide information to builders and developers
Oversee development and use of land use and zoning maps
Working relationship with P & Z Commission
Develop policy and procedure recommendations for P & Z Commission
Develop plan for impact fees

Inspections, Code Enforcement &Permitting

Establish and maintain staff
Develop, implement and maintain:
- plan review process
- building permit process
- code enforcement process
- soil erosion & sedimentation control
- certificates of occupancy

PUBLIC WORKS

Power

Generation
Distribution

Water & Sanitation

Water treatment & storage
Water distribution
Waste water collection & treatment
Biosolids treatment & handling
Water reuse/recycling

Funding & Grant Applications

Identify, pursue and manage funding

Transportation

Maintain and improve roads & bridges
Street design
Design traffic control systems
Maintain traffic system & all signals and lighting
Maintain street lights, sidewalks, gutters & related areas

Rights of Way & Facilities

Coordinate transfer of rights of way
Establish and maintain ROW permitting process
Maintain ROW's & public properties

Parks & Recreation

Manage recreation programs
Maintain park spaces & facilities

The prevalent argument that the author hears against the Public/Private partnership concept for existing cities, does not address the efficacy of the P/P/P model, but asserts that "there is no way that it can happen" for political reasons.

Let me offer some other "there is no way's" that we have heard in the past three years.

* "There is no way that you can start a new city of 90,000 people in just a few months"

* "There is no way that you can start a fully operational city with no authority, no funds and no staff"

* "There is no way that a new city can be started without an increase in taxes"

* "There is no way that a company will provide the massive resources required to start a city without a contract"

* "There is no way that you can start a fully operational city that will have less than $3 million in annual revenue"

* "There is no way that that a private company can stretch to serve more than one city"

This is just a sample of the "no ways", and all were proven wrong.

It is the author's opinion is that those who do not believe that exiting cities can (1) benefit from the Public Private partnership model, and (2) be convinced to consider the benefits, are also wrong.

A number of other myths have grown up with regard to Public/Private partnerships. A few common misunderstandings are provided in the following table:

Separating Myths from Facts Regarding Public-Private Partnerships	
Myth	**Fact**
City services can/should only be provided by the government	City services should be delivered using the most efficient and effective means possible, usually through a combination of public and private sources.
Property taxes and will be increased	The city retains authority – along with the public – for establishing property taxes.
Costs will go up	The cost of service will likely go down when services are provided by the private sector
Massive layoffs will follow in the wake of public-private partnerships	Partnerships typically protect jobs where there are existing employees involved
Service and quality will deteriorate	Most service contracts require the private partner to meet or exceed existing levels of service. In most cases, the private partner must also meet established performance metrics.
Local governments sacrifice control by working with the private sector	The public partner establishes policy, retains control as the owner of the assets, and actually increases control by having a definitive scope of service and performance measures
P/P/P's are the same as privatization	They're not the same. Privatization is the transfer of public assets to private ownership. P/P/P's are contractual relationships that provide services.

It is obvious that the benefits of partnerships can not be realized until there is progressive leadership that is willing to give consideration to a new approach.

C. TARGET CITIES

Initially, the cities that offer the best opportunities for conversion to Public/Private partnerships are in the medium to small category. That group may be defined as having a population of 250,000 or less. The reasons for the focus on cities of that size are that:

(1) politically, it will be easier to gain the needed support.

(2) smaller operations are less complex to assimilate.

The vast majority of cities in the country are of less than 250,000 in population.

It should not be inferred that the author believes that larger cities can not be converted. Not true, it is simply that the job of selling and implementing the concept will be tougher.

It is interesting that studies have shown that the optimum size for a city, on a cost per capita basis, is in the 100,000 to 150,000 population range. Even in the "most efficient" range, there is still the opportunity to improve substantially with the employment of the Public/Private partnership model.

Many larger cities already outsource a number of services to private industry. Typically, this is accomplished by competitive bidding for a specific, narrowly defined, service. When this approach is taken, a great many of the benefits obtainable from a true Public/Private partnership are lost.

It might be assumed that this type of outsourcing is a natural progression toward a P/P/P. Instead, it may prove to be a hindrance. Doubters of the P/P/P concept may use the less than optimal performance of narrow outsourced contracts to argue against a real P/P/P.

In spite of the obstacles, there seems to be a growing realization at the local, and even some state, governments that the P/P/P concept may offer advantages.

D. CONVERSION METHODS

Once an existing city has given serious consideration to a Public/Private partnership, the obvious question is: "What are the steps to accomplish the conversion?" As usual there is no "cookie cutter" method. Each city will have unique needs and circumstances. However, some actions may be offered in all cases. Additionally, we can start by identifying two distinct categories of cities.

The first type of city will be those already contracting to have a major portion of services provided by another government. Typically, this would be found in smaller cities that contract with the county or a nearby larger city.

In many ways, the conversion to a Public/Private partnership will be similar to starting a new city. The process will be one of transferring the contract from one entity to another. The fact that the elected officials, statutes and codes are already in place will make the conversion less complex than in a startup situation. The officials of such a city might benefit from referring to the book, *Creating the New City of Sandy Springs* to gain a better understanding of the process.

The second category, and the more difficult, will be cities currently providing the majority of services with internal resources.

Before beginning to outline the stages of conversion, the author should point out that the material up to this point has been based on experience. The following observations, while inferred from the measures taken and results in the new cities, are the authors recommended processes. No actual conversions of existing cities have been observed as yet. There are cities in various stages of converting to Public/Private partnerships that have not yet completed the process.

With that caveat, here are the broad steps for conversion.

1. Evaluate the community's needs and desires in every service category.

Before any effort is expended to select the private partner, the city should assess and prioritize the needs of the community, the current level of service and effectiveness, and the financial capability to meet these needs. This analysis will form the basis for negotiating the Public/Private partnership. The data will provide both the city and the company(s) with a realistic understanding of the job to be done.

2a. Evaluate the existing employees.

Employee positions and performance should be evaluated by the city. This data should be shared with the private partner(s) at the appropriate time. The private partner will then match the current employee base with the city's future needs, and with personnel available through other sources.

2b. Evaluate existing assets.

The city's assets should be evaluated. This evaluation should be provided to potential private partners and/or companies interested in acquiring assets through Privatization. (note: Privatization and P/P/P are two separate processes.)

2c. Desired service levels

The city should provide guidance with regard to service expectations, levels of effort, etc.

3.Preliminary service plan.

Based in part on the above procedure, the private partner should create a preliminary plan for providing the desired services with consideration to available financial resources.

4.Negotiate (sole source or bid process) a contract.

Based on the preliminary service plan, an agreement on the partnership may be reached which will include the financial terms and a final plan for service.

5. New management team in place in parallel to existing management.

The private partner will assemble a new management structure (which may include existing managers) to begin working with the city to facilitate the transfer of services.

6a. Hire employees.

Selection of existing city employees and hiring of new employees needed to accomplish the service plan.

6b.. Identify sub contractors.

It is very likely that the private partner will require a number of sub-contractors to provide the full array of services. The private partner remains as the city's single point of contact as the managing partner, and is fully responsible for the services.

7. Training

Begin training of new employee team (new and existing)

8a . Install and test new systems.

New systems may be required to improve performance and efficiency. Compatibility with existing systems must be assured. Employee training on new systems begins.

8b. Activate new systems in parallel.

To the extent possible, any new or modified systems should be loaded with data and activated in parallel to existing systems to assure a smooth transition.

9. Contracts with subs.

Final identification and activation of the sub-contractors occurs at this point.

10. Transfer assets

Any city assets that are required to be utilized in the provision of contracted services should be transferred, or financially accounted for, in the contract. Other assets of the city that are not a part of the service contract will be retained by the city and may be considered for privatization.

11. Fully operational

The private partner assumes full responsibility for the citt's services under the contract.

Sequence of steps:

```
_I____I____I____I_____I____I____I____I____I____I____I
(1)  (2a)  (3)  (4)    (5)   (6a) (7 )  (8a)  (9) (10)  (11)
  (2b)                     (6b)        (8b)
```

The time between step (1) and (11) will vary by city depending on the size of the city and the numbers of services being converted. In general, the process should take no more than six months from beginning to end.

A suggestion is that the conversion time line should not begin in an election year, or immediately after an election. City officials need to be able to give this concept their full attention. After all, it is probably the biggest decision that will be made in their time of service. Midterm is probably the most desirable time to commence the conversion.

The following is offered as a guide to the material that a city should be prepared to share with any company that is proposing a Public/Private partnership.

Existing General Material

Demographics
Maps
Master plan
Feasibility studies
Comprehensive plan
Capital improvement plans
Governance structure

Scope of Services

Services to be contracted (public works, community development, administration, etc.)
Facilities or assets include in scope
Equipment & furnishings include in scope
Computer systems and software in place
Desired level of service and/or metrics by service
Community priorities for each service
Organization chart
List of employees in affected service areas

Agreements

With other agencies (governments, developers, Improvement districts, etc.)
Franchises (cable, power, telephone, etc.)

Financial

Budget
Summary of projected revenues and costs
Annual reports for three years

E. SELECTING A CORPORATE PARTNER

Once the decision has been made to proceed toward a Public/Private partnership, the single most important action is the selection of the company to be the city's partner. All of the decisions on contract stipulations, service criteria, and even costs, should be secondary to identifying a company that the city feels that it can trust. So long as there is a feeling of true partnership all of the benefits outlined throughout this writing can be realized. Lack of trust and cooperation will be a major detriment to finding the best path to excellence.

Unfortunately, although there are a number of companies that should have the capability to provide the complete range of core services, at this early stage of the introduction of Public/Private partnerships, there are few companies that can exhibit such experience. As the concept spreads, there will undoubtedly be more companies that enter the field. The advent of new competitors for the cities' business will be a healthy development. However, as the new competitors emerge, cities should be aware that there will be a learning curve for new entrants. A city should consider some general factors in choosing the best partner.

* The company should have experience, or be able to demonstrate the ability, to manage the full scope of city services.

* The company as a top priority should determine the needs of the community as a basis for its proposal. Any firm that indicates a desire for the business without completing this vital determination should be given little consideration.

* The company should indicate that it has either formed, or plans to form, a business unit devoted to serving cities. This is a step toward assuring the city of a long term commitment, and will also influence the company's need to succeed to make the partnership a success.

* The company should show true enthusiasm for undertaking such a complex project. The desire to restart the city with a "clean sheet" for innovation and productivity gains should be evident

* The company must have the financial ability to back up its commitment to the city. A strong balance sheet and income history are vital.

Because of the priorities listed above, the best method for an existing city to arrive at a contract may be a sole source, or negotiated contract. In this method the city can focus on the priorities and have the greatest opportunity to understand the company's willingness and capability to meet the cities needs.

If a competitive bid process is the preferred method of selecting a private partner, the reader may wish to refer to review the earlier book *CREATING THE NEW CITY OF SANDY SPRINGS* which contains substantial information on the Request for Proposal (RFP) process. In evaluating responses to the Requests for Proposals that Sandy Springs issued, the city placed more emphasis on the factors listed above than on costs. Every city will need to establish its own criteria for selecting a corporate partner; but the Sandy Springs criteria may be of interest.

The evaluation was based on a point score with a maximum possible score of 400 points. There were four major components of the score, each counting for 100 points. Within three components there was a further breakdown. The fourth component, the contract cost, was based on a formula.

Specifically the four components were:

1. *Qualifications* - an examination of the firm's capacity to serve and financial position.

2. *Experience* - Previous experience with providing specified services.

3. *Implementation* - detailed methods and timeline for implementing the city's services/functions by the due date.

4. *Financial* - the company's cost proposal

The following formula was utilized:

The low bid was awarded 100 points.
Points for higher bids were awarded as follows:

A ratio of the low bid dollars to the higher bid dollars was calculated and multiplied by 100.

$$\frac{\text{Low Bid}}{\text{Higher Bid}} \times 100 \text{ Points} = \text{Bid points}$$

This evaluation method is provided to illustrate the emphasis placed on factors leading to mutual trust rather than a more rigid "low bidder " selection.

In the future, it might be preferable to place additional weighting on the third element: *Implementation*

F. FREQUENTLY ASKED QUESTIONS

It might be useful at this point to provide some of the more frequently asked questions concerning the transition from a traditional city to a Public/Private partnership.

Q: What is the best form or model of government delivering services?
A: There are several options, including a traditional form of service; a hybrid form of some city employees and some outsourcing; or a more entrepreneurial approach using a public-private partnership.

Q: If we do transition to a P/P/P, what are the steps we should take?
A: Carefully develop a plan that assures financial viability through understanding of revenues and expenses. Select a partner and jointly develop a comprehensive transition plan.

Q: Is a public-private partnership the same as privatization?

A: No, Although the terms public-private partnership and privatization often are used interchangeably, they are not identical. Privatization typically means the transfer of public assets to private industry. The public private partnership is the transfer of operating and service responsibility to private industries.

Q: Why would a newly incorporated city hire a private company to manage the city?

A: There are several reasons and benefits for hiring a private company:

- Expertise, experience, and resources
- Business systems, tools, and processes
- Lower cost
- Risk transfer
- Financial assistance for startup of a new city or township
- Contractual performance obligations
- Avoidance of long-term liabilities associated with employee pensions and capital cost of assets

Q: Can a private company really do it cheaper since it is profit-oriented?

A: Yes. A private company typically can save anywhere from 15 to 30 percent versus a traditional public-employee model of government.

Q: Do we lose control if we hire a private company?

A: No. A city may actually increase its control because it has a contract with clearly defined, scope of work, performance criteria, obligations and penalties to which it can hold its partner accountable.

Q: Why would a municipality want to hire a company to perform work normally done by public-sector employees?

A: Over the past decade there has been a growing trend towards implementing public-private partnerships as a way to secure services and infrastructure at lower costs. Municipalities are increasingly under intense pressure to deliver services for the lowest cost possible. A private company can draw upon resources not available, or as accessible to the public sector. Also, with no established bureaucracy, a newly incorporated municipality has the advantage of starting with a "clean sheet of paper" in determining its preferred service delivery model.

Q: What services has the private sector typically provided to cities under a public-private partnership?
A; Municipalities across the country have been employing public-private partnerships for decades to deliver many services to their citizens. These include water, wastewater, solid waste collection and disposal, snow removal, street maintenance, and many other public works functions. Adding "city hall" functions is simply an extension of a highly successful and thoroughly proven service delivery model.

Q: Can existing municipalities change from a public-sector service delivery model to a private-sector service delivery model?
A: Most municipalities have the ability to deliver a wide range of services through public-private partnerships. Changing from an existing public-sector delivery model to a private-sector delivery model is a major decision; therefore, we expect that many established municipalities will closely observe this new approach to "city hall" operations before inaugurating any change - unless they are faced with some significant challenges and feel that the time is right to move in a new direction.

Q: How can a private-sector company assure a municipality that it is always acting in the best interests of the municipality?
A: The cornerstones of the contracts that have been drawn are transparency and accountability to the cities. We know from experience that a company will be successful if it delivers the best possible service and value to the citizens.

Q: How might a city feel comfortable that it is getting the best service and value from its private-sector partner?
A: These service partnerships are developed in a very competitive business environment. Performance can be readily compared with other communities of similar size.

Q: If a city decides to enter into a public-private partnership, can it revert to a public service delivery mode at a later date?

A: Public-private partnerships are set up to allow municipalities to withdraw from a contractual relationship at the end of a contract term or to even terminate a contract prior to its end date for justifiable cause. It is important to note that the overwhelming majority of municipalities that enter into public private partnerships choose to remain in them because of the high quality of service, flexibility and value they have been able to achieve and maintain through this approach.

CHAPTER VII

It is a world of startling possibilities
-Charles Fletcher Dole

INTERNATIONAL

The author was somewhat surprised that interest in the Sandy Springs model could come from countries outside the United States. However, upon reflection, it is only natural that cities worldwide would have an interest in more effective government. After all, economic principles and the need for superior citizen satisfaction are universal.

Financial requirements are basically the same and very simple:

(1) Revenue should be at least equal to costs

(2) Assets should be at least equal to liabilities

This is true in the U. S.; and it should be true elsewhere.

Citizen satisfaction is even more simple. Local government should strive to understand the needs of the citizens and provide services that the citizens desire in the most efficient manner.

If these criteria are met, good government will be forthcoming.

A. JAPAN

The author was asked recently to visit Japan as the guest of Toyo University, under the sponsorship of the Ministry of Education and Science. The purpose of the visit was to assist in introducing the Sandy Springs model of Public/Private partnership to leaders of local governments in Japan.

The Ministry has provided a substantial grant to the University to investigate PPP's and to begin to introduce the concept to Japanese cities if it appeared to be a superior method. Professor Sam Tabuchi and Professor Nemoto spearheaded the initial effort. Working with limited resources – primarily graduate students- these two academic leaders have assimilated a good understanding of the methodology and benefits of the PPP model.

After visits to Sandy Springs and other cities in the United States, an exploratory team invited the author to Japan to assist with the introduction of the concept. Major symposia were held in Tokyo and Osaka.

In Tokyo, before an audience of 500 government, business and academic leaders, the author had the opportunity to recount the PPP experience of Sandy Springs and other Georgia cities. As related in earlier sections, that experience has been remarkable.

A number of smaller meetings and press conferences were held providing opportunities for in-depth discussions. The questions indicated a good grasp of the concept by many of the participants. There appeared to be significant interest in the application of the model in Japan. Several leaders expressed a desire to have their city be the first to actually introduce the Public/Private partnership.

In America, local government has been operating the same way for over a hundred years. It should be obvious for that reason alone, that change should be considered. After all, what else has been unchanged for such a long period? In America, in one hundred years, we have seen the advent of automobiles, airplane travel , radios, televisions, computers and even space travel, yet the method of providing services by local governments is basically unchanged.

Japan, as a much older country, is even a better candidate for reevaluation.

Unfortunately, it often requires a crisis before political leaders are willing to consider change. It appears that many local governments in Japan are approaching a financial crisis. As requirements for public disclosure of finances are being implemented, the very shaky condition of many cities is becoming evident. For example, one large area is acknowledging a deficit of $50 billion with no obvious way to rectify the situation if present policies and traditional methods continue. Their deficit as a percentage of income is enormous. The U. S. federal deficit, as large as it is (related to GNP) is miniscule compared to their financial problem.

With this background, local government leaders may be willing to consider the Public/Private partnership model.

In addition to the author, representatives of CH2MHill, the leading private partner in providing PPP services to local government in the United States, also participated in the conferences. Their description of the service and cost advantages available in the Sandy Springs model seemed to strike a receptive chord with the Japanese leaders.

The principal question that the leaders raised was whether the P/P/P principles introduced in the new city of Sandy Springs could be applied to existing cities in Japan. The short answer was a resounding "Yes!". In many ways, it is easier to convert an existing city than to create a wholly new operation. The obvious reason is that the personnel, systems, equipment and facilities are already in place. It becomes a matter of transitioning these elements to a more efficient management system. This is not to imply that the transition is simple; but, from a technical standpoint, it is far less complex than starting a city with no resources in place.

Just as in America, the major hurdle to overcome is political. There is a structural resistance to change and a distrust of new methods that cannot be ignored. In many cases it is as detailed in Chapter V, a "knee jerk" reaction with little basis in fact. In addition, there will be opposition from individuals and groups that feel that their self interests are being threatened. Again Japan does not appear to differ from the U. S. in this regard.

The major "anti" elements will likely flow from such special interest groups as employees, who are naturally concerned about their jobs, and businesses, suppliers and developers, afraid of losing a favorable relationship with the city. While these concerns are rational, they are based more on fear than reality.

The most frequently asked question in our meetings dealt with the concern for the future of existing city employees. Japan has a long history of employee security and laws that protect employment. While the overriding responsibility of government is to its citizens and not the employees, there is a need to deal with employees as fairly as possible. To that end, the representatives of CH2MHill described their past experience and practices in establishing Public/Private partnerships. Senior Vice President Gary Miller offered the following explanation regarding options for existing employees.

> *Those of you who have dealt with any type of outsourcing or public-private partnership know when existing employees are involved it is very important to define how those individuals will be affected. Where a newly incorporated City is created, there may actually be no employees and the private partner provides all the personnel to perform the contracted services. However, in the case of an existing city that chooses to outsource, the situation is different. There are several options to consider where existing employees may be affected. These include:*
>
> *1) The City and the private partner agree to a plan to make employment opportunities available to all existing employees. In this case, the City may share in the solution by allowing employees*

near retirement, or with a certain level of tenure, to transfer into other open City positions. The private partner also participates by hiring the remaining employees to perform the work it has not contracted for.

2) The City requires that the private partner hire all affected employees. This is also a viable option; but the private partner then likely needs time (1-3 years) to affect the type of organization change and efficiency gains expected by the municipal government.

3) The City terminates the employment of those affected employees before the private partner begins. This is the least attractive option since it has a negative impact on the affected individuals and also is not a politically viable option for City leadership. While this is an option, it is rarely if ever used because of the negative implications.

In summary, successful public-private partnerships require a win-win-win solution for the City, its employees, and the private partner. By taking a long-term view of efficiencies and improved service levels that can be gained, options for existing employees to ensure they have continued career opportunities can be defined. The private partner will typically offer employment to affected employees in comparable positions and with comparable pay and benefits, so that existing staff are motivated and willing to make a successful transition".

In short, there are no "cookie cutter" solutions. Every city should customize its plans for the transition of employees, based on the current situation. The author reiterates the position that it is not the job of government to provide jobs, but rather, to serve the needs of the citizens as efficiently as possible. Sometimes hard decisions are necessary.

Given Japan's need for an immediate improvement in the financial position of its local governments, there is an obvious opportunity for the introduction of PPP's in many cities.

With a financial burden of great magnitude, such as the $50 billion deficit in one area, many actions must be taken to begin to ameliorate the situation in addition to converting to a P/P/P.

A couple of old adages might apply: "to heal a wound you must first stop the bleeding", and "if you are in a deep hole, stop digging". Before the debt can be reduced, one must first stop running deficits. This is what the conversion to a P/P/P can do. Simultaneously, existing debt must be reduced. The author, while not an authority on such steps, can offer some thoughts.

In Chapter I, the difference between a P/P/P and Privatization was discussed. Both concepts may be needed to attack a severe debt problem, P/P/P to stop the bleeding due to inefficient operations, and Privatization to effect a rapid reduction in the debt. With Privatization, the city's assets may be sold to private companies, resulting in immediate cash to repay debt. In addition, depending on the contract, there may an income stream associated with the sale. Many cities may be surprised at the assets that are owned, and not only have value to a company, but also may enhance the city's revenue if properly developed. Examples could be:

1. "Air Rights" in which developers can build major facilities above existing structures.
2. Privately owned structures that provide municipal parking.
3. Private structures that house transportation Facilities

Some of the more common Privatization efforts in the U. S. include Public Utilities and Toll Roads

Certainly, this is but a small list of possibilities for Privatization. The ingenuity of private industry to create opportunities is often amazing.

Local governments have problems that will be difficult to turn around; but a continuation of "business as usual" is not the answer. The hole will only get deeper. There are solutions, through a partnership with private industry, but there must exist the political will to take the necessary actions, and not to delay the process.

The service in hotels, restaurants and other public places in Japan is marvelous. A combination of this service culture - with the creativity, resources and technology available through private industry - should result in great improvement in local government.

To effect the needed changes, Japan needs some Heroes.

It is hoped that by the time this book is published, one or more trials of Public/Private partnerships will be in the preliminary stage. Ideally, these trials should be in cities of 25,000 to 100,000 population. A city of this size will be sufficient to offer impressive results but be less complex to convert than a large city. In the larger cities, trials that convert a single service or department may be an acceptable initial phase. Keep in mind that while conversion on a departmental basis should offer some improvement, the optimum gains will occur with a broad conversion, such as provided in the Sandy Springs model.

Chapter VIII

I shall try to correct errors when shown to be errors, and I shall
adopt new views so fast as they shall appear to be true views
- Abraham Lincoln

CONCLUSION

There is no question that the Sandy Springs model of Public/Private partnership has been a success for the new cities. There is also no reason to believe that this model will not work as well for existing cities. The transition period must be handled with skill and sensitivity; but, once that experience is completed, the clear benefits of citizen satisfaction and improved financial condition will be realized.

Considering the growing positive results with the Public/Private partnership model, it is imperative that every city should, at the very least, give consideration to the potential benefits that are available.

No decision of this magnitude should be made without proper consideration. A commitment to preliminary fact-finding is a reasonable first step. Even a very cursory comparison such as the cost per capita for comparable services will suffice to exhibit the benefits, or not, of the P/P/P model.

Government in the United States is on a dangerous path. Spending at the federal level is out of control. Many states are experiencing increasing financial difficulties. It is well beyond the experience of this writer to be able to offer solutions for these massive problems. But I have seen enough to offer hope at the local government level.

The economic strength of this country has always been our private industry. The desire of our people to excel, to create and innovate, has been the engine that has driven the U. S. to a position of world leadership. It is now time that we look to private industry for solutions to the creeping bureaucracy, stagnation and inefficiency that plagues so many of our cities.

It should not be enough for our local leaders to try to manage the existing system to the best of their abilities. The citizens need leadership that is willing to break the mold of traditional methods and give genuine consideration to a better model.

Somewhere out there are such leaders. It is upon their shoulders that our hope for better government lies.

This book is a clarion call for such American heroes.

If you want to be a hero, call me, I am in the book.

Oliver W. Porter
Sandy Springs, Georgia

oliverporter1@comcast.net

APPENDIX A

PROPOSAL FOR A PHASED STUDY OF THE OUTSOURCING OF MUNICIPAL SERVICES IN THE UNITED STATES

Prepared by the Center for Advanced Communications Policy, Georgia Institute of Technology

James D. White, Ph.D.
Paul M.A. Baker, Ph.D.

Summary

The revival of interest in the adoption of outsourcing of municipal services (aka "contract government") has attracted attention across the nation. While this interest is naturally highest among communities considering incorporation, many existing cities and other localities are also considering the potential benefits of outsourcing all or a part of their operations to private sector service providers. The relative novelty of the concept of municipal service outsourcing, especially in the comprehensive model currently at work in the city of Sandy Springs, Georgia, means there is a dearth of factual data and a consequent lack of analysis of the efficacy of such a model. At the same time, the very newness of the model offers a unique opportunity to build baseline data and develop such an analysis, including a comparison with 'traditional' municipalities, allowing for a clear understanding of the relative merits and demerits of the two concepts.

This proposal offers a phased approach to building a comprehensive, comparative analysis and review of the outsourcing of municipal services in the U.S. Note that each level is dependent on the successful completion of, and incorporates the work of, the level(s) preceding it.

Level One encompasses a review of the literature on the subject, and a compilation of baseline data available from accessible public and other secondary sources, focusing on some key variables in selected areas (such as financials, demographics) and limited to five case studies.

Level Two introduces a comparative element to the compilation of baseline data, by expanding the research sample to include five "traditional" cities, selected on the basis of geographic and demographic comparability to the contract cities. Technology adoption and implementation is introduced. The comparison serves as the basis for exploring the outcomes of outsourcing.

Level Three is a major expansion of the activities, to include developing and conducting surveys across the case cities. The key questions of citizen satisfaction and accountability are introduced.

Level Four takes advantage of the newness of the model to develop an assessment through time, allowing for the survey model developed and initially conducted in Level 3 to be further developed according to feedback and conducted in an ongoing periodic fashion over a span of three years. This Level would also encompass a Delphi survey of acknowledged authorities in the field of government, administration and outsourcing, who, on the basis of the compilation of data and of the survey results would be asked to brainstorm future developments.

1. PURPOSE OF THE PROPOSED STUDY

Previous work on outsourcing[0] to some extent focused on cost savings and efficiencies. There is a substantial body of research that has documented significant savings for government or society at large[1]. But it was President Reagan, an early proselytizer for public-private partnerships, who reminded us that they should be designed to accomplish social goals. Ultimately government is about citizen interaction, and a key measure of success is about the extent to which the interaction is successful or not. The relative novelty of the models of municipal service outsourcing that will be the focus of this study offers a unique opportunity to develop a clear picture of the relative merits and demerits of the concept, allowing us to see what indeed are "best practices," including questions of use of technology, of communication, and of political participation. The aim is to develop optimal approaches to government.

2. RESEARCH QUESTIONS

The ultimate research question is to determine, through a comparative study of contract and traditional cities, what are the relative merits and demerits of the concept of municipal service outsourcing, what may be learned from that comparison, and how might those lessons be applied to develop optimal approaches to government

For the purposes of this proposal:
"Contract" is defined as cities in which the majority of services other than public safety are provided by the private sector.
"Traditional" is defined as cities in which the majority of services are provided by employees of the municipality.
The reference points for the research questions will include

---

[0] See "Privatization: Lessons Learned by State and Local Governments." United States General Accounting Office, March 1997
[1] See "Cost Savings from Privatization." John Hilke. Reason Foundation, March 1993

The relative financials and demographic data (Level One). Note: in cooperation with the partners in the research it will be necessary to clarify, what specifically are we trying to ascertain? Are we interested in efficiency gains? Based on output/citizen; tax dollar saving/citizen; or community aggregate?

The relative use of technology (Level Two). Note: in cooperation with the partners in the research we will clarify in what capacity: for example, back office processing; municipal service management; communications; online permit issuing, etc.)?

The relative degree of citizen satisfaction and input (Level Three). Note: in cooperation with the partners in the research it will be necessary to clarify whether this refers to comparative across the target cities, or to a benchmark?

In the course of the research, and as the phases are implemented in sequence, it is inevitable that other reference points will emerge, such as the relative presence or absence of liabilities such as benefits or depreciation. Another example might be the notion of the relative flexibility of resources. In this case "Flexibility" indicators might attempt to ascertain the degree to which both personnel and assets may be redeployed or shifted to meet both short and long term needs in an efficient manner.

3. METHODOLOGY

Data collection will be undertaken via several methods dependent on the specific question and the phase of the research.

Level 1: Baseline. The sample frame consists of 5 case cities[2]. For the majority of the work in this exploratory research study we expect that a compilation of secondary resources would be the most effective. The focus will be on "hard" data, in particular demographic and financial

[2] these are initially Sandy Springs, GA; Johns Creek, GA; Milton, GA; Weston, FL; and Centennial, CO; the list may change subject to findings of literature review)

data. Financial data will be aggregate indicators compiled from appropriate secondary sources which may include: annual reports, city budgets, contracts, financial data filed with the states.

An important part of the work of Level 1 would be the development of questionnaires for use in Level 2, and early identification of potential candidates for the role of "traditional" control cities, to be carried out in Level 2.

Level 2: Baseline/Comparative Analysis. The sample frame is expanded to introduce the comparative element. It will consist of 5 case cities (see note below), and 5 control cities, to be determined. Control ("traditional") cities will be selected for geographic and demographic comparability to the contract cities. Control cities should offer comparable services, or adjustments should be made for missing services.

We will distribute questionnaires to key city stakeholders, and work to ensure their timely completion, tabulate and analyze the results. As one example, technology adoption and deployment will be explored via a questionnaire which will be developed by us and directed to stakeholders/policymakers in the sample cities (see notes above with respect to specific questions under evaluation). Technology adoption and deployment indicators will be developed based on literature reviews and consistent with target objectives. The resulting instrument will ascertain the current level of utilization and attempt to estimate the municipalities' ability to meet future developments.

We anticipate conducting some interviews, primarily for clarification rather than as a primary data source.

Level 3: Baseline/Comparative Analysis/Primary Data Collection This phase represents a major expansion of the activities, to include developing and conducting surveys across the case cities, and a much closer engagement by the research staff with the subject matter, including a series of in-depth interviews. This expanded focus will add depth and richness to the comparisons, allowing for an understanding of the real make-up of the different municipalities, looking at political,

economic, and social settings. This will also allow for insight into the key questions of citizen satisfaction and accountability. Citizen satisfaction should include metrics (to be determined) for a defined number of specific services such as: City operations, Public works, Transportation, Permitting, Parks, Police, Fire, Responsiveness, Accessibility, Ability to provide input to city, and more. Citizen satisfaction levels will be developed in the first place based on existing secondary sources, followed by specific, targeted assessment surveys.
This phase will include a travel budget to allow for a research team to visit out-of-state comparison municipalities, and conduct in-person interviews and research.

Level 4: Baseline/Comparative Analysis/Primary Data Collection/ Longitudinal Study. This phase would permit the an assessment through time, as it would allow for the survey developed and initially conducted in Level 3 to be further developed according to feedback and conducting in an ongoing periodic fashion over a period of three years. The aim here would be to develop a reference model for municipal services, allowing interested parties to see and weigh the variables, and take into account tradeoffs in terms of available budgets, resources, differences in local culture, history and geography, and so on. This Level would also encompass a Delphi survey of acknowledged authorities in the field of government, administration and outsourcing, who, on the basis of the compilation of data and of the survey results would be asked to brainstorm future developments.

4. OUTPUT/DELIVERABLES

Please note that the projected delivery dates indicated below may change according to the date of the actual contractual arrangement between CACP and the Reason Foundation.

Level 1 Deliverables:
Results of the Level 1 exploratory research study will be compiled into an overview/assessment report addressing the 5 case cities (Sandy Springs, GA; Johns Creek, GA; Milton, GA; Weston, FL; and Centennial,

CO.), encompassing demographic and financial data from appropriate secondary sources.;
Questionnaires will be developed for subsequent use in Level 2;
There will be preliminary identification of candidates for the role of "traditional" control cities, to be carried out in Level 2. Projected delivery date: April 30, 2008.

Level 2 Deliverables:
A summary report will be generated presenting follow-on work from Level 1 including assessment and surveys of the control ("traditional model") cities selected for geographic and demographic comparability. As one example, technology adoption and deployment will be explored via a questionnaire that will be developed by staff and directed to the sample cities.
An experimental model will be developed to test some of the assumptions with respect to the current level of utilization and estimate the municipalities' ability to meet future developments. Projected delivery date: September 15, 2008.

Level 3 Deliverables: This phase represents a major expansion of the activities, and deliverables will include
Development and administration of surveys across the target and control case cities;
A series of in-depth interviews and the collection of primary "satisfaction" and accountability data (both remotely and "onsite");
Development of a comprehensive cross-sectional "picture," that allows for comparative analysis and identification of critical distinctions between target and control cities; and an initial set of "best practices" and recommendation for enhanced governance efficacy based on the findings of the research study. Projected delivery date: November 31, 2008.

Level 4 Deliverables:
Longitudinal Study: development of an outsourcing "observatory" reporting on the results of surveys administered in an ongoing periodic fashion over a three-year period;

Conduct of a Delphi survey of acknowledged authorities in the field of government, administration and outsourcing, who, on the basis of the compilation of data and of the survey results would be asked to brainstorm future developments;
Development of a reference model (and assessment instrument) for municipal services. Projected delivery dates semi–annually, 2008 – 2010.

5. OUTLINE BUDGET

(Budget section has been deleted)

APPENDIX B

(Note – this sample is derived from the RFP of a new city with a Public/Private partnership. It is an excellent guide for a new city. It should be a good guide for an existing city that plans to convert to a P/P/P. There are certain elements such as the transfer of data from the county etc. that will need to be deleted. Additional elements will most likely be needed to deal with such issues as the transfer of personnel from the city to the company, and with the specific needs of the issuing city that differ from the model.

CITY of______________________________

REQUEST FOR PROPOSAL

FOR

PROVISION OF ADMINISTRATIVE, FINANCIAL COMMUNITY SERVICES, EMERGENCY 911, PHYSICAL PLANT, MOTOR VEHICLE, STAFFING, AND PURCHASING, PROCUREMENT, CONTRACTING SERVICES, PUBLIC WORKS, TRANSPORTATION, STREETS, RIGHT-OF-WAY, FACILITIES, PARKS AND RECREATION, CAPITAL IMPROVEMENTS, PLANNING AND ZONING, INSPECTIONS, CODE ENFORCEMENT, AND PERMITTING

TO THE CITY OF ______________________

PROPOSALS OPENED: (time) (date)

INSTRUCTIONS TO PROPOSERS

All the spaces below and in the attached Proposal Signature and Certification form are to be filled in with signatures supplied where indicated. Failure to sign Proposal will cause rejection of your proposal.

PROPOSAL OF:

COMPANY
NAME:
ADDRESS:
SUBMIT PROPOSAL TO;

____

(NAME)

____

(ADDRESS)

PROPOSAL MAILED:
CARRIER USED:

NOTE: **PLEASE ENSURE THAT ALL REQUIRED SIGNATURE BLOCKS ARE COMPLETED. FAILURE TO SIGN THIS FORM WILL CAUSE REJECTION OF YOUR PROPOSAL**

Issuer

PROPOSAL

We propose to furnish and deliver any and all of the services named in the attached Request for Proposal (RFP). The price or prices offered herein shall apply for the period of time stated in the RFP.

This offer is being made with knowledge that the City of ___________ is promulgating this RFP in accordance with its authority granted by virtue of **(state statute).**
It is understood and agreed that this proposal constitutes an offer, which if accepted in writing by the City of ___________ City Council, and subject to the terms and conditions of such acceptance, will constitute a valid and binding contract between the undersigned and the City of

____

It is understood and agreed that we have read the specification shown or referenced in the RFP and that this proposal is made in accordance with the provisions of such specifications. By our written signature on this proposal, we guarantee and certify that all items included in this proposal meet or exceed any and all such specifications. We further agree if awarded a contract, to deliver services, which meet or exceed the specifications.

It is understood and agreed that any proposals shall be valid and held open for a period of sixty (60) days from the date selection of the corporation as the preferred vendor until the contract is completed. It is understood that any expenses incurred by an offeror in preparing and presenting the proposal shall be at the risk of the offeror.

______________________	______________________
Authorized Signature	Date
______________________	______________________
Print/Type Name	Print/Type Company Name

PROPOSAL SIGNATURE AND CERTIFICATION

(Offeror must sign and return with proposal)

I certify that this proposal was made without prior understanding, agreement, or connection with any corporation, firm, or person submitting a proposal for the same materials, supplies, equipment, or services and is in all respects fair and without collusion or fraud. I understand collusive bidding is a violation of State and Federal Law and can result in fines, prison sentences, and civil damage awards. I agree to abide by all conditions of the proposal and certify I am authorized to sign this proposal for the offeror.

______________________	___________________
Authorized Signature	Date
____________________	_________________
Print/Type Name	Print/Type Company Name

1.0 GENERAL INFORMATION

1.1 Introduction

Pursuant to its authority granted by virtue of (state statute), the City Council of the City of_________ is requesting proposals for Provision of Services to the City of________, (the "City") to implement, manage and operate a wide range of services/functions for the city to be initiated on Jan 1,____. This RFP is issued pursuant to its authority granted by virtue of (state statute) and subject to all of the terms, limitations, and conditions as set forth therein. Competitive sealed proposals shall be submitted in response hereto. All proposals submitted pursuant to the request shall be made in accordance with the provisions of these instructions.

As set forth herein, there shall be mandatory pre-proposal conference of all bidders. Further, packaging of bid services is allowed for the purposes of this Request for Proposal ("RFP"), provided however, that each component of said packaged services must be individually detailed in said response. Offerors may, and are encouraged, to form partnerships regarding the provisions of any particular services set forth herein to insure that the City has benefit of the best possible team to provide the required services.

The proposals shall be evaluated in accordance with the evaluation criteria set forth in this RFP. Subsequent to the opening of the sealed proposals, discussions may be conducted by the City Council with responsible offerors who submit proposals for the purpose of clarification to assure full understanding of and responsiveness to the solicitation requirements. Offerors shall be accorded fair and equal treatment with respect to any opportunity for discussion and revision of proposals.

In conducting any such discussion, there shall be no disclosure of any information derived from proposals submitted by competing offerors. All such discussions shall be conducted by a committee comprising some or all of the Council members.

In accordance with (state statute), the Council may make decisions, taking into consideration qualifications, experience in provision of similar services, price, identification of potential needs, thoroughness of proposals, and all other evaluation factors set forth in this RFP. No other factors or criteria shall be used in the evaluation. The Council reserves the right to reject any and all proposals submitted in response to this request and to withdraw this RFP at any time.

1.2 **Background**

The City is considering the adoption of the Public/Private model for the provision of services within the City. At the time that the contract may be initiated the City will have a population of approximately ______ ____________residents and the Council is soliciting these proposals to evaluate the most cost effective, efficient, and reliable method of meeting a broad range of needs for the City.

With this model, the City intends to implement one of the most effective, efficient and responsive local governments in the State of ________. The Council believes that creative solutions are available that can produce effective government for the 21st century.

Foremost among these solutions is tapping the resources of private industry through contracting for services and functions. Our desire is to identify firms that can provide a wide variety of services allowing the city to deal with a limited number of contracts. Further, we are seeking firms that have had experience in providing services/functions to other municipalities, or as a minimum, to similar entities.

While it may be necessary to contract with the other governments for some services, the intent is to keep that to a minimum. A successful contractor will have the opportunity to showcase the firm's capability in serving the needs of municipal governments.

With the aforementioned restrictions on contracts and spending, the Commission must establish a relationship of trust with potential contract firms. The recommended firms must be financially able and willing to, in the months preceding the start date, establish the infrastructure, hire and train staff, and undertake any functions that will be necessary for the city to operate from its inception.

1.3 **Timetable**

The following timetable is anticipated for this RFP:

____________	Release of RFP
___________	Mandatory Pre-Proposal Conference
_____________	12:00 p.m. Proposals due
_____________	Oral Presentations if required)
_____________	Evaluation Recommendation, if any (on or about)

Proposals will be received at the date and time set forth above in the following location:

(Name)
(Address)

1.4 **Restrictions on Communications with the City Council**

1.4.1 Until a provider is selected and the selection is announced, offerors are not allowed to communicate for any reason with any member of the City Council or representative concerning this RFP except through the Officer named herein, or during the pre-bid conference. For violations of this provision, the Council shall reserve the right to reject the proposal of the offending offeror.

2.5 **RFP Amendments**

1.5.1 The Council reserves the right to amend the RFP prior to the deadline for proposal submission, ________. Amendments will be sent to all offerors who originally received a copy of the RFP. If an RFP amendment will impact the timeline contained in Section 1.3, all offerors will be promptly provided information concerning any timeline revisions.

1.6 **Proposal Withdrawal**

1.6.1 A written proposal is not subject to withdrawal except that, prior to the proposal due date, a submitted proposal may be withdrawn by the offeror submitting a written request to the Officer named herein. Any such request must be signed by a person authorized to sign for the offeror.

1.7 **Costs for Preparing Proposal**

1.7.1 The cost for developing the proposal is the sole responsibility of the offeror. The City will not provide reimbursement for such costs.

1.8 **Contract Term**

1.8.1 The contract will be a multi-party contract between the service provider and the City. The term, if any, of the contract shall commence on ________, and shall terminate on _________, except that the Contract shall automatically renew for five (5) additional twelve (12) month periods unless affirmative written notice of non-renewal is given by the City not less than thirty (30) days prior to the expiration of the instant term. The terms and construction of the Contract shall be governed by applicable (state) law.

1.9 **Contract**

1.9.1 The Contract, which the Council intends to use with the successful offeror, is attached as Attachment "A" to this RFP. Prospective offerors are urged to carefully read the Contract prior to making their offers. The Contract and any exceptions to the provisions of the Contract must be submitted with the offeror's proposal. The Council reserves the right to negotiate with the successful offeror other additions to, deletions from and/or changes in the language in the Contract, provided that no such addition, deletion or change in the contract language would, in the sole discretion of the Council, affect the evaluation criteria set forth herein or give the successful offeror a competitive advantage.

The offeror shall confirm acceptance of the provisions of the Contract or, in the alternative, shall state explicitly which provisions are not acceptable and propose alternative wording or any additional wording or any additional provisions that the offeror believes to be necessary. Any exception to the Contract must be clearly identified, accompany the offeror's proposal, and be attached to the Contract. Offerors are cautioned that any exception submitted that would give the offeror a competitive advantage over another offeror or that would cause a failure to meet a mandatory requirement of the RFP will not be accepted.

Upon determination of the apparent winning proposal, offeror will be required to enter into discussions with the Council to resolve any contractual differences. These exceptions are to be finalized and all exceptions resolved within one (1) week of notification. If not, this could lead to rejection of the offeror's proposal. No exception to the Contract will be deemed to have been accepted by the Council unless the exception is incorporated by reference into the final executed Contract. The Council reserves the right to make non-material revisions to the form of the Contract as necessary at any time.

1.10 **Offers by One or More Partners**

1.10.1 Offerors may, and are encouraged, to form partnerships regarding the provisions of any particular services set forth herein to insure that the City has benefit of the best possible team to provide the required services. If more than one partner is participating in any response, however, each partner shall respond separately regarding their individual businesses, including but not limited to all responses to the RFQ portion of this request. All responses will further clearly delineate the specific responsibilities and duties of each partner regarding the requested services.

1.11 **Format for Responses**

1.11.1 Proposals should correspond with and satisfy the requirements set forth in this RFP. The offeror must submit the original proposal plus _____ copies of its proposal to the Council. Proposals should be in one sealed package marked clearly on the front, "City of ________ RFP "

1.12 **Additional Information**

1.12.1 An offeror that submits a proposal that meets the requirements set forth in this RFP may be requested to provide additional information or to meet with representatives of the Council to discuss the specifics of the proposal in greater detail.

1.13 **Retention of Proposals**

1.13.1 All material submitted in response to this RFP will become the property of the Council and may be returned at the option of the council. One copy shall be retained by the council for official files.

1.14 **Waiver of Irregularities**

1.14.1 The Council reserves the right to waive any irregularities of any proposal submitted for this RFP.

1.15 **Questions about this RFP**

1.15.1 Questions regarding the requirements or technical criteria set forth in this RFP should be directed in writing to the individual listed below. The response and the question will then be shared with other offerors who are responding to this RFP.

Name: ______________________
Address: ______________________
Telephone: ______________
E-mail: ______________________

The deadline for the submission of these questions is 12:00 P.M. __________. Questions should reference the appropriate RFP section and may be submitted by email. Any files attached to e-mails must be MS Word format.

2.0 REQUEST FOR OFFEROR QUALIFICATIONS/ ASSURANCES

2.1 Required Qualifications and Information

The Council deems that it is in its best interest to work with offerors that have proven capabilities with a well-established record of success in the provision of the type of services being requested hereunder. To that end, the offeror shall include in a separate envelope as set forth herein, the following:

2.1.1 Offeror's name, address, and telephone number.

2.1.2 Primary local contact person(s) and telephone number(s).

2.1.3 Total number of offerors's full-time employees designating the geographic location of said employees with representative numbers regarding said location.

2.1.4 Year established.

2.1.5 Provide a listing and description of all current litigation involving the offeror.

2.1.6 Provide a listing and description of all litigation history for the offeror with any claim in excess of Twenty Thousand and 00/100 Dollars ($20,000.00) since and including the most recent 15 years.

2.1.7 Provide a copy of the most recent completed year's financial statements (Income Statement and Balance Sheet) for the offeror.

2.1.8 List of all projects similar in quality and/or scope to that set forth in this RFP– Include: size, cost, total fee, implementation time, scope of services, awards received, and brief description of project.

2.1.9 Provide a description of the offeror's special capabilities, techniques or resources that can be contributed to this assignment. A minimum of three (3) references from projects of a similar scope and type shall be submitted with each proposal by offeror. Particular emphasis should be placed on demonstrating previous experience with projects for municipalities. Describe the offeror's, and/or proposed team's, qualifications to complete the work. The planning and/or expertise required to accomplish the complete scope-of-work must be represented either within the offerror's in-house staff, or by a partnership of offerors. A partnership submission must be made by an offeror. If the submission is a partnership submission, describe the previous experience that the offeror has had working with the various partners. Identify and provide resume information for the project manager and the key personnel who will be involved in implementing the project.

2.1.10 Statement of offeror's capability to absorb additional workload, availability of personnel, and commitment to provide services on a timely basis.

2.1.11 Conflict of Interest Statement.

As a duly authorized representative of________________ _______________ I, ____________________________ with the title ____________________________, certify that to the best of my knowledge that no circumstance exist which will cause a conflict of interest in performing services for the City of __________, that no employee of ______________, nor any public agency official or employee affected by this Request for Qualifications has any pecuniary interest in the business of this firm, associates or consultants of this firm, or the firm's parent firm, subsidiary, or other legal entity of which this firm is a part, and that no person associated with or employed by this firm has any interest that would conflict in any way, manner or degree with the performance of services for the City of _________.

Date: ____________________

Company Name:___________________________

Authorized Representative Name: __________________________________

Title: ___________________________________

Signature: ________________________________

2.1.12 Provide a proposed Organizational Chart which identifies individual names and areas of responsibility regarding the implementation and responsibilities of the duties hereunder.

2.1.13 Provide a comprehensive outline of the steps you propose in order to meet the services required by this RFP. This detail should indicate what is to be done, who individually, and by name is responsible to do it, and when it is to be completed.

2.1.14 At your option, you may provide any additional supporting documentation or information which would be helpful in evaluating your qualifications and commitment.

2.1.15 The proposal should contain any documents pertaining to the requirements mentioned above and any other information the offeror deems necessary to fully demonstrate the offeror's qualifications so as to allow the council to evaluate the offeror's ability to provide the services requested herein.

2.2 **Proposal Guaranty**

2.2.1 No proposal will be considered unless it is accompanied by a proposal guaranty in the form of a cashier's check, a certified check, a savings and loan secured check, or a bid bond payable to the City of ________ in the amount of five percent (5%) of the total bid to ensure that the successful offeror will execute the contract which it has been recommended and ultimately awarded by the City. The proposal guaranty shall be forfeited by an offeror who fails to execute promptly and properly the contract it has been awarded, or who fails to furnish the required performance security and certificate of insurance in their proper forms within the time requirements indicated in this RFP. **ALL PROPOSAL GUARANTY SHALL BE RETAINED UNTIL FINAL CONTRACT AWARD.**

2.3 **Council**

2.3.1 Upon notification of the Council's selection, the apparent successful offeror shall furnish, within ten (10) days, a performance bond in the amount of one-hundred ten percent (110%) of the proposal amount on a form prescribed by the Council. Failure to furnish a bond within ten (10) days may result in rejection of the proposal, forfeiture of the proposal guaranty, and awards of the contract to another offeror. Additionally, for a performance bond surety to be acceptable to the Council as surety for performance bonds, a surety company shall comply with the following provisions:

2.3.2 The surety company shall be authorized by law to do business in the State of _______ pursuant to a current certificate of authority to transact business issued by the Commissioner of Insurance.

2.3.3. The surety company shall be on the United States Department of Treasury's list of approved bond sureties.

2.3.4. All bonds shall be signed by a (state) Licensed Resident Agent who holds a current power of attorney from the surety company issuing the bond.

2.3.5. PERFORMANCE SECURITY SHALL BE RETAINED BY THE CITY OF __________ FOR A MINIMUM OF 150 CALENDAR DAYS FROM THE DATE OF CONTRACT COMPLETION.

2.4 **Financial History**

2.4.1 The Council reserves the right to evaluate the financial integrity of the offeror. Prior to the award of the contracts, all offerors shall be required to submit the following items:

2.4.1.1 Audited Financial Statement or 10K Report for the most recent two (2) years, including at minimum:

2.4.1.1.1 Statements of income and related earnings;

2.4.1.1.2 Cash flow statement;

2.4.1.1.3 Balance sheet;

2.4.1.1.4 Opinion concerning financial statements from a CPA.

2.4.1.1.5 Primary banking source letter of reference.

2.5 **Customer Reference**

2.5.1 The offeror must provide the names of customer references, including a specific contact name and phone number of any entity to whom the provider has ever provided the proposed service or a similar service.

3.0 REQUIRED SERVICES

3.1 General

3.1.1 The services required for which this RFP is being issued shall include but not be limited to those outlined in Sections 4.0 et seq. through 14.0 et seq. hereof. The intent of the Contract is that the offeror firm assumes full responsibility for the structure, planning, and implementation necessary to provide the required services to the City. Where the offeror anticipates needs that may occur which are not specifically set forth hereunder, the offeror is expected to identify with specificity those needs as part of its proposal. The intent of the Contracts is that the offeror firm assumes full responsibility for the structure, planning, and implementation necessary to provide the required services to the City. Where the offeror anticipates needs that may occur which are not specifically set forth hereunder, the offeror is expected to identify with specificity those needs as part of its proposal.

3.1.2 It is anticipated that the proposal submitted hereunder shall, if awarded, be incorporated as an addendum to Exhibit "A" of the Contract between the offeror and the City to further define the scope of the offeror's services thereunder. Accordingly, all responses should be in a format suitable for incorporation into said Contract as an exhibit.

3.1.3 All services and duties must be operational as of the date of the award of the Contract by the City, should the City decide to make such award.

3.1.4 Each of the following shall include as a material provision thereof the attendance as necessary and/or requested of any an all meetings of the City Council to either discuss and/or make recommendations regarding any matters within the purview of the requested services. Whenever the requirement calls for the offeror to develop and/or implement a policy, it shall be material provisions thereof that such policy shall be made in furtherance of the directives as provided to the offeror by the City Manager.

4.0 CITY ADMINISTRATIVE, FINANCIAL, AND COMMUNITY SERVICE REQUIREMENTS

4.1 ADMINISTRATIVE SERVICES

4.1.1 Administrative services shall include, but not be limited to the following.

4.1.2 **Contract Administration**

4.1.2.1 Assist the City Manager in negotiating City contracts, as directed by the City Manager.

4.1.2.2 Advise the City Manager on the status of negotiations as well as contract provisions and their impacts on the City.

4.1.2.3 Make recommendations on contract approval, rejection, amendment, renewal, and cancellation, as directed by the City Manager

4.1.2.4 Provide contract administration and supervision of all contracts, as directed by the City Manager.

4.1.2.5 Ensure ongoing protection of City interests.

4.1.2.6 Ensure compliance with all laws related to bidding, contracting and purchasing as set forth in the State of ___ _______.

4.1.2.7 Assist and coordinate any necessary grant applications and submissions as directed by the City Manager.

4.1.3 **Policy Implementation**

4.1.3.1 Research current and likely future trends impacting the City.

4.1.3.2 Prepare administrative and financial analysis of all available options.

4.1.3.3 Attend all City Council meetings, hearing and agenda meetings, as directed by the City Manager.

4.1.3.4 Assist City Manager with identification of significant policies and analyze their administrative and financial impacts.

4.1.3.5 Prepare plans and procedures to ensure implementation of the City Council policies and directives, as directed by the City Manager.

4.1.3.6 Prepare status reports to advise the City Manager of the progress and results of public policy implementation.

4.1.4 **Daily Communications**

4.1.4.1 Respond to all inquires as directed.

4.1.4.2 Prepare correspondence regarding City affairs for the City Manager and City Clerk, as requested.

4.1.4.3 Ensure compliance with all Open Records and Open Meetings laws as set forth in state statutes

4.1.5 **Customer Service**

4.1.5.1 Provide first-tier response to customer inquiries.

4.1.5.2 Establish response protocols and direct customers to the appropriate party.

4.1.6 **Departmental Support**

4.1.6.1 Provide overall administrative support of all City functions and departments.

4.1.7 **Clerking Support**

4.1.7.1 Record and transcribe all City Council meetings, hearing and agenda meetings.

4.1.7.2 Assist City Clerk during Council meetings, take attendance, record motions and votes taken, and swear in witnesses of others presenting testimony to the Council.

4.1.7.3 Assist in the review of documents to be presented to the Council, as directed by the City Manager.

4.1.7.4 Upon City Clerk's absence, authenticate all City documents by appropriate signatures and City Seal.

4.1.7.5 Retain public records and make them available for inspection by the public, in conformance with (state) law.

4.1.7.6 Prepare all Council meeting agendas.

4.1.7.7 Publish all appropriate public notices.

4.1.7.8 Serve administrative needs of any and all Boards, Authorities or other entities established by the City for the furtherance of City objectives.

4.1.8 **Records Management**

4.1.8.1 Implement and maintain a custom-designed, state-of-the-art Document Management System to facilitate creating and saving all documents into the system (Word & Excel), then archiving these documents.

4.1.8.2 Improve employee productivity, collaboration, and document security by allowing the users to search for documents by profile information, content, person who created them, or even last person to edit the document. Users may also modify a previously created document for their use while leaving the original document unmodified.

4.1.8.3 Provide sufficient document scanning stations in City Hall so that any and all paper documents such as signed contracts, ordinances, resolutions, and other important City documents may be imported into the Document Management System using the Document Scanning Station.

4.1.8.4 Protect integrity of all public records in accordance with the requirements of State law.

4.1.8.5 Promote sharing of information and collaborative work between all City staff.

4.1.8.6 Provide an application server that will store and manage required data.

4.1.8.7 Provide and maintain access to data for other City contract providers as necessary.

4.1.8.8 Design state-of-the-art storage strategies and systems for all public records. Implement and coordinate the transfer of any and all necessary data, records, or other materials as necessary for the operation of the City. This requirement must be met at the time of the award of the Contract by the City, if any.

4.1.9 **Public Relations**

4.1.9.1 Maintain continuous dialog and communications with City residents with timely updates, as directed by the City Manager.

4.1.9.2 Promote City policy, programs and achievements.

4.1.9.3 Serve as a liaison with residents, civic groups and other governments, as directed by the City Manager.

4.1.9.4 Document important City events for future use in City-developed publications.

4.1.10 **Annual Reports**

4.1.10.1 Develop a graphical and thematic design theme for the Annual Report, for approval by the City Manager.

4.1.10.2 Coordinate with the graphic designers, photographers, editors and others as necessary.

4.1.10.3 Provide effective written and non-written communications to reflect the year's message and inform residents of the City's actions and achievements.

4.1.10.4 Produce, print and deliver the annual reports to City residents.

4.1.11 **City Website**

4.1.11.1 Design and host the City website containing City contact information, statistics, history, departmental and facility description, Council meeting schedule, meeting agendas, agenda packages, minutes, City Codes, notices, and City in pictures and multimedia.

4.1.11.2 Update the site daily to post latest agendas, packages and minutes, notices, etc. and redesign the site annually.

4.1.11.3 Publish City-provided GIS database interface on the website.

4.1.12 **City Newsletter**

4.1.12.1 Provide text, pictures, graphics, maps, exhibits, etc. as necessary for the quarterly newsletter.

4.1.12.2 Coordinate with the publishers to produce a useful, informative, timely and attractive publication.

4.1.12.3 Produce, print and deliver a quality newsletter to all City residents.

4.1.13 **Program Presentation**

4.1.13.1 Publish studies, reports and analysis for staff and public presentation, as directed by the City Manager.

4.1.13.2 Prepare various media presentations of City programs to the staff and general public, as directed by the City Manager.

4.1.14 **Information Technologies and Telephone Systems**

4.1.14.1 Provide, install and maintain state-of-the-art information technology, software and hardware sufficient to efficiently satisfy all City needs.

4.1.14.2 Provide a state-of-the-art domain network to account for handling future growth and technologies.

4.1.14.3 Provide, install, configure and maintain a state-of-the-art server at City Hall and all City offices to improve performance ensure against data loss and minimize potential down time.

4.1.14.4 Provide centralized management of all network resources and a central location for the storage of the City's documents.

4.1.14.5 Ensure data security and integrity with a nightly backup (with offsite storage) and the ability to restore from a central location.

4.1.14.6 Provide, configure and maintain _____ state-of-the-art laptop computers to Mayor (1) the members of the City Council (_), City Manager (2), and City Clerk (1).

4.1.14.7 Provide, install, configure and maintain state-of-the-art computer workstations, as needed.

4.1.14.8 Provide digital phones and remote connections for park sites.

4.1.14.9 Maintain software and hardware uniformity and interchangeability among users.

4.1.14.10 Provide, install and maintain sufficient network laser printers to efficiently conduct all City business.

4.1.14.11 Maintain a three-year replacement program for all computers and equipment.

4.1.14.12 Provide, install and maintain state-of-the-art network cabling/data line system for communications, networking and data sharing.

4.1.14.13 Provide, install, configure and maintain servers in support of utility functions.

4.1.14.14 Provide all users with Internet and e-mail connections on a separate server for internal and external communications and common contact lists and scheduling.

4.1.14.15 Archive all e-mails in compliance with State retention requirements.

4.1.14.16 Provide, install and maintain a state-of-the-art telephone system in all City facilities with sufficient lines and features to satisfy all needs of the City.

4.1.15. **Databases – Municipal Management Software**

4.1.15.1 Provide, install, configure and maintain a state-of-the-art database program to manage the City's occupational and business license functions

4.1.15.2 Coordinate the procurement, installation, configuration and maintenance of all databases required of municipalities in the State of _________by any governmental agencies.

4.1.16 **Court Services**

4.1.16.1 Provide all aspects of court record keeping and reporting as required by law and sound practices including but not limited to maintenance of calendars, recording of sentences and dispositions, coordination with probation services, coordination of collection of fees, fines and surcharges.

4.1.16.2 Provide administration personnel for Court hearings

4.1.16.3 Oversee and maintain all systems required for fee, fine and surcharge accounting, reporting and remittance.

4.1.17 **Police**

4.1.17 Provide administrative and clerical assistance in all aspects of police department record keeping and reporting as required by law and sound practices in coordination with City authorities.

4.1.18 **Fire**

4.1.18 Provide administrative and clerical assistance in all aspects of fire department record keeping and reporting as required by law and sound practices in coordination with City authorities.

4.1.19 **Election Support**

4.1.19.1 Coordinate municipal and special elections as required, including but not limited to addressing polling station issues, preparation of ballot questions, or other related issues arising from election matters.

4.1.20 **Solid Waste**

4.1.20.1 Manage and coordinate all aspects of agreements with solid waste providers.

4.2 **FINANCIAL SERVICES**

4.2.1 Financial Services shall include, but not be limited to the following.

4.2.1 **Revenue Collection**

4.2.1.1 Coordinate with local, state and federal agencies charged with collection and disbursement of taxes, assessments, fees, charges and other impositions.

4.2.1.2 Administer the fees, charges and their miscellaneous revenues pertaining to utilities, private enterprises and individuals as they interface with the City programs.

4.2.1.3 Recommend enforcement actions to the City Manager to induce payment in accordance with the City's policies and procedures.

4.2.1.4 Prepare monthly financial reports showing revenues and expenses to date in comparison with budget projections and submit the reports to the City Manager no later than the tenth day of the following month.

4.2.1.5 Maintain a City address list for the Department of Revenue to ensure that the City obtains all shared revenues to which it is entitled.

4.2.2 **Capital Program Administration:**

4.2.2.1 Coordinate with the designated city representatives the capital needs of the City.

4.2.2.2 Obtain financing if necessary and maintain proper fund accounting procedures.

4.2.2.3 Administer and implement capital program financing.

4.2.3 **Investment Services**

4.2.3.1 Recommend investment policies and procedures pursuant to State law.

4.2.3.2 Invest City funds per approved policies.

4.2.3.3 Produce timely investment reports stating the effectiveness of the chosen investment policy.

4.2.4 **Fund Accounting**

4.2.4.1 Establish Fund Accounting System in accordance with Governmental Accounting Standards Board (GASB), the Uniform Accounting System prescribed by Department of Community Affairs and the rules of the state Department of Audits and Accounts.

4.2.4.2 Prepare reports for Department of Community Affairs and State Revenue Department and distributions.

4.2.4.3 Prepare all other financial reports as required by applicable law and accounting standards.

4.2.5 **Accounts payable/receivable**

4.2.5.1 Administer the purchase order system and make timely payment of all invoices.

4.2.5.2 Coordinate tax collection, franchise fees, utility taxes and all other receivables.

4.2.6 **General fixed asset accounting**

4.2.6.1 Account for assets constructed by or donated to the City for maintenance.

4.2.6.2 Inventory City property in accordance with GASB and the state Department of Audits and Accounts.

4.2.7 **Budgeting:**

4.2.7.1 Prepare and submit to the City Manager annual budgets per GASB standards.

4.2.7.2 Liaison with all City departments for annual budget categories.

4.2.7.3 Provide material for and attend all budget meetings, hearing and agenda meetings.

4.2.7.4 Coordinate with other departments and governmental entities as necessary.

4.2.7.5 Present findings in oral, print, multimedia, and web-based forms.

4.2.8 **Forecasting:**

4.2.8.1 Prepare detailed financial forecasts and analysis.

4.2.8.2 Identify trends and analyze their impact upon City's finances, operations and capital.

4.2.8.3 Develop policy and action recommendations.

4.2.8.4 Coordinate with other departments and governments.

4.2.8.5 Present findings in oral, print, multimedia, and web- based forms.

4.2.9 **Comprehensive Annual Financial Report (CAFR):**

4.2.9.1 Prepare the Annual Financial Report for Units of Local Government, in accordance with Generally Accepted Accounting Principals as defined by the Government Finance Officers Association.

4.2.10 **Risk Management:**

4.2.10.1 Recommend and advise the City Manager of the appropriate amounts and types of insurance and be responsible for procuring all necessary insurance.

4.2.10.2 Process and assist in the investigation of insurance claims, in coordination with the City Attorney.

4.2.10.3 Develop and maintain a risk management claims review procedure, in coordination with the City Manager and City Attorney.

4.2.10.4 Review insurance policies and coverage amounts of City vendors.

4.2.11 **Human Resources:**

4.2.11.1 Ensure proper functioning of payroll, fringe benefit, insurance tax and other City-specific and general law-provided human resources functions.

4.2.11.2 Establish a Code of Conduct for personnel that emphasize the responsibility of the staff to be professional, patient and responsive under all circumstances. The Code should emphasize that rudeness and impoliteness toward any person is unacceptable conduct and will not be tolerated.

4.2.11.3 Establish and implement with all employees an Employee Policies and Procedures Manual, which shall include, but not be limited to, policies and procedures on carrying out duties to the City, consequences of non-compliance to policies, and functions and roles of the employees.

4.2.12 **Purchasing:**

4.2.12.1 Recommend to the City Manager and assist in the implementation of procurement policies and procedures.

4.2.12.2 Assist in selection of vendors.

4.2.12.3 Participate in county and state level purchase plans.

4.2.12.4 Prepare RFP's, as directed by the City Manager.

4.2.12.5 Prepare and process requisitions.

4.2.13 **HIPAA**

4.2.13.1 Ensure that all City systems and procedures meet the requirements of HIPAA.

4.3 **COMMUNITY SERVICES**

4.3.1 **Water Management and Utilities:**

4.3.1.1 Manage and coordinate all aspects of intergovernmental relationship regarding water and sewer issues.

4.3.2 **Animal Control**

4.3.2.1 Provide field staff for the daily maintenance of animal control issues in the City.

5.0 **EMERGENCY 911 SERVICE**

5.1 **Emergency 911 Infrastructure and Staffing**

5.1.1 The offeror shall be responsible for coordinating with the County on the provision of Emergency 911 system for the City.

6.0 PHYSICAL PLANT REQUIREMENTS

6.1 Office, Administrative and Facilities Space

6.1.1 The offeror shall be responsible for providing facilities sufficient for the operations of all departments and functions the City on the date of acceptance of the proposal, whether or not offeror is responsible for said operations or function, if the Contract is awarded to offeror by the City. All space shall meet all minimum GSA requirements, and exhibit a level of finish customary for a local government. Should offeror be the lessee of such space, offeror must have complied with all requirements for leasing said space as required by local governments under state law, the lease shall be at a fair market value rental rate, and such lease shall provide for an unconditional assignment of such lease to the City of ________ exercisable by the unilateral determination of the City. Should offeror be the owner of such space, offeror shall allow the City of ________ the option to purchase said property at fair market value, with such option exercisable by the unilateral determination of the City. Should the City assume any lease, or purchase any property as contemplated hereunder, there shall be no rent required of the offeror for the use of the space hereunder so long as said space is being devoted to purposes of the City. It is anticipated that the successful offeror will consult with the Board pursuant to the terms set forth in this RFP, including at the Mandatory Pre-Proposal Conference, to coordinate the most beneficial space taking into consideration, cost effectiveness, location in the City, and other relevant factors.

6.2 Facilities Maintenance, Repair and Contracts

6.2.1 The offeror shall be responsible for providing personnel to maintain, repair, clean, and keep in good working order all facilities commensurate with local governmental standards all facilities occupied by the City. This provision, however, shall not apply to landscaping maintenance of any City rights-of-way or land.

6.3 **Furniture, Fixtures, Equipment and Supplies**

6.3.1 The offeror shall be responsible for providing Furniture, Fixtures, Equipment and Supplies in an amount sufficient for the reasonable operation of all departments and functions the City on the date of acceptance of the proposal, whether or not offeror is responsible for said operations or function, if the Contract is awarded to offeror by the City.

7.0 **MOTOR VEHICLE REQUIREMENTS**

7.1 The offeror shall be responsible for providing Motor Vehicles sufficient for the operations of all departments and functions the City on the date of acceptance of the proposal, whether or not offeror is responsible for said operations or function, if the Contract is awarded to offeror by the City. This requirement shall exclude any specialized service related emergency vehicles such as Police and/or Fire Emergency Vehicles; however the requirement will include sufficient vehicles for administrative necessities of said police and fire personnel.

7.2 The offeror shall submit a detailed Motor Vehicle Use and Safety Policy for the use of such vehicles by any staff of offeror sufficient to ensure that the City is protected regarding the use of said vehicles.

7.3 The offeror shall further be responsible for all maintenance, inspections, and other necessary service regarding said motor vehicles.

8.0 **PUBLIC WORKS**

8.1 Public Works services shall include, establishing, staffing (as needed to meet the requirements herein), and maintaining the Public Works Department for the City. The areas of responsibility shall include, but not be limited to, the following:

8.1.1 **Storm Water**

8.1.1.1 Coordinate with all other City personnel and/or contractors the transfer maintenance, storage and retrieval of all documents and records necessary for the effective implementation and operation of the City's storm water requirements under applicable, federal, state, and local laws. The offeror shall be responsible for determining the documentation necessary for transfer as well as coordinating and implementing the physical retrieval, reproduction and storage of the transferred records.

8.1.1.2 Provide ongoing engineering, design and maintenance of storm water systems, as needed, to meet the needs of the City.

8.1.1.3 Develop and implement all necessary policies, protocols, rules and regulations necessary to meet or exceed the City's storm water requirements under applicable, federal, state, and local laws, including but not limited to federal clean water requirements.

8.1.1.4 Integrate activities as necessary with Planning/Zoning and other departments.

8.1.2 **Emergency Preparedness**

8.1.2.1 Establish policies and guidelines, and coordinate, operate and maintain the city's emergency preparedness program in accordance with all applicable, federal, state, and local laws, as well as prudent local government practices.

8.1.2.2 Integrate and coordinate all emergency preparedness operations in conjunction with Homeland Security, Emergency 911, FEMA, and GEMA.

8.1.3 **Recycling**

8.1.3.1 Establish policies and guidelines, and operate the city's Recycling program.

8.1.3.2 Coordinate implementation of program and all other activities with City personnel and/or contractors.

8.1.3.3 Fulfill all reporting duties as required by any federal, state or local laws.

8.1.4 **Geographic Information System (GIS)**

8.1.4.1 Coordinate with all other necessary City personnel and/or contractors the transfer, maintenance, storage and retrieval of all documents and records necessary for the effective implementation and operation of the City's GIS System. The offeror shall be responsible for determining the documentation necessary for transfer as well as coordinating and implementing the physical retrieval, reproduction and storage of the transferred records.

8.1.4.2 Service, update and maintain GIS data bases on not less than a monthly basis.

8.1.4.3 Provide any GIS related information and/or data in response to requests and needs of City personnel as well as any other contractors.

9.0 **TRANSPORTATION**

9.1 Transportation services shall include, establishing, staffing (as needed to meet the requirements herein), and maintaining the Transportation Department for the City. The areas of responsibility shall include, but not be limited to, the following:

9.1.1 **Funding and Grant Applications**

9.1.1.1 Conduct all activities necessary to identify, develop and prepare submissions for any federal, state or local funding and grant programs, and provide fund oversight as required by law.

9.1.2 **Traffic Engineering**

9.1.2.1 Conduct all activities necessary to maintain a first quality traffic system, including but not limited to, conducting necessary studies and implementation of traffic control improvements.

9.1.3 **Street Design**

9.1.3.1 Conduct all activities necessary to maintain a first quality street system plan, including but not limited to, the coordination, review, and management of all contracts for streets, sidewalks and related projects.

9.1.4 **Street Maintenance**

9.1.4.1 Conduct all activities necessary to maintain a first quality roadway and bridge infrastructure system, including but not limited to providing necessary maintenance of all roadways and bridges, which shall include minor repairs, cleaning, and repairs necessitated by storm events. The offeror may provide this service by the use of subcontractors, provided however, when subcontracts are anticipated, the offeror should include as part of its proposal the same information regarding said subcontractor as required of offeror in Section 2.0 hereof. Offeror should further provide an estimate of annual costs for the services of said subcontractor as a separate section of the quotation submitted on this RFP.

9.1.5 **Street lights, Sidewalks, Gutters and Related Street Areas**

9.1.5.1 Conduct all activities necessary to maintain first quality street lights, sidewalks, gutters and related street areas including but not limited to providing a necessary maintenance and cleaning of the same. The offeror may provide this service by the use of subcontractors, provided however, when subcontracts are anticipated, the offeror should include as part of its proposal the same information regarding said subcontractor as required of offeror in Section 2.0 hereof. Offeror should further provide an estimate of annual costs for the services of said subcontractor as a separate section of the quotation submitted on this RFP.

10.0 **STREETS, RIGHTS-OF-WAY, AND FACILITIES**

10.1 **General**

10.1.1 Streets, Rights-of-Way, and Facilities services shall, in addition to the requirements set out in Section 6.2, include, but not be limited to, establishing, staffing (as needed to meet the requirements herein), to:

10.1.1.1 Establish, operate and oversee all aspects of the City Rights-of-Way permitting process.

10.2 **Contract Administration.**

10.2.1 Establish, operate and oversee all aspects contract administration for daily maintenance of all public rights-of-way and property, including but not limited to landscaping and irrigation systems, in order to provide safe and comfortable common grounds for the residents of ______ ______.

10.2.2 Establish, operate and oversee all aspects contract administration for the construction, operation and maintenance of public facilities.

10.2.3 Establish, operate and oversee all aspects of emergency preparedness plan with local, state and federal agencies for debris removal, roadway access, flood prevention and safe, operable utilities.

11.0 **PARKS AND RECREATION**

11.1 Parks and Recreation services shall include, establishing, staffing (as needed to meet the requirements herein), and maintaining the Parks and Recreations for the City. The areas of responsibility shall include, but not be limited to, the following:

11.1.1 Plan, implement and coordinate staffing and contract administration for the daily maintenance and use of all public parks and recreational facilities.

11.1.2 Plan, implement and coordinate staffing for the planning, promoting, and supervising of recreation programs and special events.

11.1.3 Plan, implement and coordinate staffing for the managing, coordinating and scheduling of City athletic facilities as needed.

11.1.4 Develop and recommend to the City Manager short, mid, and long-range plans for capital improvements and implement plans as directed.

11.1.5 Establish, operate and oversee all aspects of emergency management procedures with local, state and federal agencies to ensure safe recreational system.

11.1.6 Conduct all activities necessary to identify, develop and prepare submissions for any federal, state or local funding and grant programs for improvements to the park and recreation system within the City, and provide fund oversight as required by law.

12.0 **CAPITAL IMPROVEMENTS**

12.1 Develop and recommend to the City Manager short, mid, and long-range plans for capital improvements and implement plans as directed. Such plans should meet all requirements of the Department of Community Affairs and the _________ Regional Commission for adoption in the City's Comprehensive Land Use Plan.

13.0 **PLANNING AND ZONING**

13.1 Planning and Zoning services shall include, establishing, staffing (as needed to meet the requirements herein), and maintaining the Planning and Zoning Department for the City. The areas of responsibility shall include, but not be limited to, the following:

13.1.1 Provide information to the general public as it relates to all land development activities within the City.

1231.2 Provide information to builders and developers regarding policies and procedures within the City related to land planning within the city.

13.1.3 Oversee the development, maintenance and updating of land use and zoning maps as required by state and local agencies.

13.1.4 Develop policies and procedures regarding all planning and zoning activities, and develop schedules and time frames for processing all land development activities (including, but not limited to, zoning).

13.1.5 Provide information to the City Manager, Mayor and Council, Planning and Zoning Boards, and any other City entities needing information regarding all relevant and applicable zoning and/or planning issues.

13.1.6 Develop, plan, recommend and implement, in coordination with all other City staff or contractors, a plan for the implementation and assessment impact fees by the City.

13.1.7 Conduct all activities necessary to maintain a first quality planning an zoning system for the City.

13.1.8 Develop, plan, recommend and implement, in coordination with all other City staff or contractors, a plan for the issuance of certificates of use and occupational licenses.

14.0 INSPECTIONS, CODE ENFORCEMENT, AND PERMITTING

14.1 Inspections, Code Enforcement and Permitting services shall include, establishing, staffing (as needed to meet the requirements herein), and maintaining the Inspections, Code Enforcement, Permitting Departments for the City. The areas of responsibility shall include, but not be limited to, the following:

14.1.1 Develop, plan, recommend and implement, in coordination with all other City staff or contractors, a plan review process for the City.

14.1.2 Develop, plan, recommend and implement, in coordination with all other City staff or contractors, a plan for the building permit process for the City.

14.1.3 Develop, plan, recommend and implement, in coordination with all other City staff or contractors, a plan for the code enforcement process for the City.

14.1.4 Develop, plan, recommend and implement, in coordination with all other City staff or contractors, a plan for the authorization and implementation plan for the City to conduct Soil Erosion and Sedimentation Control inspections for the City.

15.0 STAFFING REQUIREMENTS

15.1 General

15.1.1 Offeror shall provide with the Proposal a list of the proposed staffing requirements necessary to meet the needs for each of the services, duties, and/or functions outlined in Sections 4.0 <u>et seq.</u> through 14.0 <u>et seq.</u>.

15.2 Key Positions

15.2.1 Regarding key positions, which shall include the proposed director of any department, the offeror shall provide a brief summary of said proposed key personnel's experience and qualifications for said position, provided, however that it shall be the duty of the offeror to assess the qualifications and skills of any proposed personnel and their suitability for the proposed positions. Offeror shall consider staffing recommendations of the City, should the offer ultimately be accepted by the City. In addition, the proposal shall provide for the following position(s) setting out in detail the qualifications of the candidates for the following position(s):

15.2.2 **Program Manager**

15.2.2.1 The Program Manager shall be an executive level person with the offerer. This position is not required to be full time, but is intended to provide general supervision and to assure that adequate resources are being provided to fulfill the terms of the contract.

15.3 **Assistant City Manager**

1.5.3.1 The Assistant City Manager shall have the responsibility working with the City Manager to coordinate and direct all of the activities set out in this RFP should it be accepted by the City. The Assistant City Manager will be a work closely with the City Manager and the City Council regarding all aspects of the offeror's activities should the offer be accepted by the City. Said Assistant City Manager shall be the primary coordinator of all communications between the City and the Corporation.

15.4 **Subcontractors**

15.4.1 Should the offeror intend to engage the services of any subcontractors regarding the delivery of services set forth herein, the name, address, and qualifications of such subcontractor shall be included in the proposal. Should the offeror include any subcontractors as potentially performing any of the services hereunder, the offeror shall affirmatively acknowledge as part of its proposal that the offeror shall be the sole entity to which the City shall look to for performance of the required services.

15.4 **Personnel**

15.4.1 The offeror shall include an affirmative statement in its proposal that it shall not knowingly engage in employment of, on any basis, any Council member or committee members involved in the preparation of this RFP or in the selection and/or award process of this contract during the period of this contract. Once an offeror has been selected and a service contract negotiated, the names of those staff members who participated in this RFP process shall be provided to the service provider so that the requirements of this section can be implemented.

15.5 **Employment Practices**

15.5.1 The offeror shall include an affirmative statement in its proposal shall not discriminate against any employee or applicant for employment because of race, color, religion, sex, national origin, age, marital status, political affiliations, or disability. Such action shall include, but is not limited to the following: employment, promotion, demotion, transfer, recruitment or recruitment advertising, layoff or termination, rates of pay or other forms of compensation, and selection for training, including apprenticeship. Offeror agrees to post in conspicuous places, available to employees and applicants for employment, notices setting forth the provisions of this clause.

16.0 PURCHASING, PROCUREMENT AND CONTRACTING

16.1 The offeror shall include an affirmative statement in its proposal regarding the purchasing and/or procurement of any of the items set forth or required in the course of fulfilling the duties set forth in RFP, the offeror shall meet or exceed all laws and requirements regarding the same as set forth by the State of_______ Offeror shall also meet or exceed all laws and requirements regarding the same as set forth by the State regarding any contracting required in the course of fulfilling the duties set forth in RFP.

17.0 PRICE QUOTATION

17.1 Each proposal shall include a price quote (budget) for the required services as set forth herein for the year _____, and a price for the subsequent year. Each year shall be a separate quote and meet the requirements set forth herein. The price quote for each year shall have a summary page containing a total quote for all the services requested in this RFP and a detail of the quote summarizing the components thereof in a succinct fashion. Said quote shall include a statement of the maximum increase per year for any price escalation for the agreement for the years three through six of the agreement. This quotation shall be included in Exhibit "C" to the contract, if awarded.

18.0 FORMAT OF RESPONSE

18.1 General

18.1.1 A responsive proposal shall be in accordance with Section 3.0 hereof and address each item as set forth in this RFP with specificity.

18.2 Required Sections

18.2.1 The response, shall generally follow the format as set forth below, however, the Board shall, at its discretion, waive any deviation from this format should the offeror present an alternate format which provides sufficient detail and addresses all of the requirements as set forth in this RFP:

18.2.1.1 Response to Section 2.0 et seq. Request for Offeror Qualifications/Assurances.

18.2.1.2 Presentation of proposed scope of services to conduct City Administrative, Financial and Community Service Requirements as set forth in Section 4.0 through 14.0.

18.2.1.3 Proposed staffing requirements as set forth in Section 15.0 Et.seq. The response should include a proposed organizational chart setting out the structure of the offeror's staffing plan and all other requirements as set forth in said section in detail.

18.2.1.4 A detailed start-up plan setting forth steps the offeror would take in order to meet all of the requirements for services and duties as set forth in this RFP on the date of the Award of the Contract by the City, should the City determine to award the same. The start-up plan should discuss with specificity how the proposal will meet the needs of the City. The plan should describe how the transition of services to the offeror would be accomplished. The offeror should include start-up costs when calculating the prices submitted in the Price Quotation.

18.2.2 Of the 15 copies of the complete proposal, the proposal letter on one should contain the original manual signature of the person submitting the proposal on behalf of the offeror. All 15 copies should also contain the signer's name and title typed. The proposal letter shall clearly identify the complete legal name of the offeror. Each person signing a proposal certifies that he/she is the person in the offeror's organization authorized to make the proposal. The signer shall provide his/her affiliation with the offeror, address, telephone and fax numbers.

19.0 EVALUATION AND SELECTION PROCEDURE

19.1 General

19.1.1 The Council will evaluate and select between the offerors in accordance with (state) law.

19.2 Method of Evaluation

19.2.1 The City Council will rank the proposals by virtue of a points system with points being awarded in four (4) categories as follows: (1) Qualifications and Experience, (2) Previous Experience with Similar Services and Duties, (3) Start-up and Implementation Plan,and (4) Financial.

19.2.2 The City will award One Hundred (100) potential points based on the offeror's previous qualifications and experience including a review of all of the information and documentation requested in Section 2.0 et seq. above.

19.2.3 The City will award One Hundred (100) potential points based on the offeror's previous experience in providing similar services and duties including a review of all of the information and documentation requested in Section 2.0 et seq. above.

19.2.4 The City will award Two Hundred (200) potential points based on the quality, detail, timelines and sufficiency of the offeror's start-up and implementation plan to have all of the required duties and services operational on the date of Contract Award by the City should the City decide to award the same. This analysis will also include an overall review of the entire proposal submitted by the offeror for quality, content, and detail.

Service/Function	Point Scale
Management of multi-function contracts	0 to 25
Administration	0 to 10
Accounting	0 to 10
Court support	0 to 3
Finance	0 to 8
Human Resources	0 to 5
IT	0 to 10
Police support	0 to 3
Fire support	0 to 3
Public Works	0 to 10
Transportation	0 to 10
Streets, Rights-of-Way and Facilities	0 to 8
Parks and Recreation	0 to 5
Capital Improvement Plans	0 to 5
Planning and Zoning	0 to 10
Inspections, Code Enforcement and Permitting	0 to 10
Total	0 to 100

19.2.5 The Citizens for Dunwoody will award One Hundred (100) potential points based on the relative bids.

A ratio of the low bid dollars to the higher bid dollars will be calculated and multiplied by 100.

$$\frac{\text{Low Bid}}{\text{Higher Bid}} \times 100 \text{ Points} = \text{Higher Bid points}$$

19.3 **Composite Score**

19.3.1 The sum of the points for (1) Qualifications and Experience, (2) Previous Experience with Similar Services and Duties, (3) Start-up and Implementation Plan, and (4) Financial, will comprise the Composite Score. The maximum Composite Score is 500 Points.

ATTACHMENT A

PROPOSED CONTRACT

BY AND BETWEEN

CITY OF _______, ________

AND

____

FOR PROVISION OF

ADMINISTRATIVE, FINANCIAL COMMUNITY SERVICES, EMERGENCY 911, PHYSICAL PLANT, MOTOR VEHICLE, STAFFING, AND PURCHASING, PROCUREMENT, CONTRACTING SERVICES AND PUBLIC WORKS, TRANSPORTATION, STREETS, RIGHT-OF-WAY, FACILITIES, PARKS AND RECREATION, CAPITAL IMPROVEMENTS, PLANNING AND ZONING, INSPECTIONS, CODE ENFORCEMENT, PERMITTING

THIS AGREEMENT is made and entered into this _____ day of __ ________, 200__, by and between the CITY OF _______, a (state) municipal corporation, (the "CITY"), and ____________________, a (state) corporation ("Corporation").

WHEREAS, the City is desirous of maintaining a high level of competent professional and economically feasible contract administrative, finance and community services in conjunction and harmony with its fiscal policies of sound, economical management, and

WHEREAS, Corporation has agreed to render to the City a continuing high level of professional contract services and the City is desirous of contracting for such services upon the terms and conditions hereinafter set forth, and

WHEREAS the City is desirous of providing these daily services through a contractual relationship with Corporation,

NOW THEREFORE, in consideration of the sums hereinafter set forth and for other good and valuable considerations, the receipt and legal sufficiency of which are hereby acknowledged, it is hereby agreed as follows:

Section 1. PRIOR AGREEMENTS

As of the effective date hereof, all prior agreements between the City and Corporation are terminated and replaced by the terms hereof.

Section 2. GENERAL SERVICES

2.1 Corporation shall provide to City for the term hereinafter set forth, as the same may be extended in accordance with the provisions hereof, competent services, within and throughout the corporate limits of City to the extent and in the manner hereinafter described

2.2 The City hereby engages Corporation to provide, and Corporation hereby agrees to provide, all of the services described herein and in the "Scope of Services," attached hereto as Exhibit A and incorporated herein by reference.

2.3 The parties recognize that this Agreement is intended to provide flexibility to the City in order to meet its evolving challenges. Therefore, the Corporation shall provide any and all staffing to a level necessary to all said personnel to provide professional, competent services to the City as required under this Agreement.

2.4 Corporation agrees to provide City all services and personnel necessary to fulfill the obligations of Corporation under this contract.

2.5 Except as otherwise hereinafter specifically set forth, such professional services shall encompass all those duties and functions of the type coming within the jurisdiction of and customarily rendered by municipal departments (other than those provided by other contract providers) in accordance with the Charter of the City, and the Statutes of the State of ____.

2.6 Corporation shall, at all times, foster and maintain harmonious relationships with the members of the City Council, all employees of the City, all employees of the City's contract services providers and all City's residents, and shall represent the city in the best light possible.

2.7 All communications to the Mayor, City Council and press shall be through the City Manager. All mass communications to residents shall be reviewed and approved by the City Manager prior to printing and dissemination.

2.8 The President and/or Chief Executive Officer of Corporation shall be available to meet with the City Manager at City Hall on an annual basis and at any other times at the request of the City Manager.

Section 3. FINANCIAL SERVICES

3.1 Corporation shall follow the procedures established by the City Manager for withdrawal, transfer and disbursement of City funds.

3.2 Corporation shall maintain all financial records in accordance with all applicable laws and guidelines for municipal accounting, including GAAP, GASB and GFOA standards, and shall produce and deliver to the City Manager any and all financial information and reports requested by the City Manager.

3.3 Corporation shall ensure that the City complies with all requirements regarding audits, and shall assist the City in procuring an auditor in compliance with all applicable laws and procedures.

3.4 All investments shall be made pursuant to any and all investment policies approved by the City Council in accordance with ___ ___ Statutes.

3.5 Corporation shall prepare and follow risk management policies and procedures, as adopted by the City Council.

3.6 Corporation shall take advantage of all available discounts on purchases and invoices for City purchases except when Corporation deems it is more favorable to the City based upon cash management practices.

3.7 Corporation shall promptly pay all City bills in accordance with _________ law and sound business practices.

3.8 Corporation shall assist the City in finding and applying for various grants and in fulfilling all obligations that accompany such grants.

3.9 On or before the fifteenth day of each month, Corporation shall prepare and deliver to the City Manager a monthly financial statement for the prior month.

3.10 On or before October 1 of every year, Corporation shall prepare and deliver to the City Manager an annual inventory of all City owned tangible personal property and equipment in accordance with all applicable rules and standards.

Section 4. ADDITIONAL SERVICES

4.1 Corporation shall provide to the City, upon the request of the City Manager and the availability of resources, such additional services as may from time to time be needed at the discretion of the City.

4.2 The cost of such additional services shall not be borne by the City and shall be payable in such amounts and in such a manner as may be determined by mutual agreement, upon each occurrence.

Section 5. HOURS OF OPERATION

5.1 Corporation shall maintain fully staffed business hours equal to, but not less than, the City's business hours of 8 AM to 5 PM, Monday through Friday, with the exception of the following holidays:

New Year's Day
President's Day
Memorial Day
Independence Day
Labor Day
Veteran's Day
Thanksgiving Day
Day After Thanksgiving Day
Christmas

5.2 For all City related matters, Corporation shall use the address of _________ City Hall, including both incoming and outgoing mail.

Section 6. EQUIPMENT AND LABOR

6.1 Corporation shall furnish to and maintain for the benefit of the City, without additional cost, all necessary labor, supervision, equipment (including motor vehicles excluding, however, any specialized service related emergency vehicles such as Police and/or Fire Emergency Vehicles) necessary and proper for the purpose of performing the services, duties and responsibilities set forth and contemplated herein and as necessary to maintain the level of service to be rendered hereunder. In the event of emergencies or natural disasters, Corporation shall, immediately and on and on-going basis, supply its usual and customary personnel to ensure continuing operation of all services provided by Corporation and to satisfy all County, State and Federal administrative requirements.

6.2 All City owned equipment shall be used only for City purposes in performance of this Agreement, and shall not be used for any Corporation or personal purposes.

6.3 All City owned vehicles and equipment utilized by Corporation employees shall be maintained in strict accordance with manufacturer's recommended maintenance, and Corporation shall keep full records of all maintenance. All City vehicles shall be kept clean, free of damages and in safe operating condition. All City vehicles shall be used in strict conformance with the Vehicle Use Policy attached hereto as Exhibit B.

6.4 Corporation shall comply with all OSHA and other applicable standards for work place safety. Corporation shall comply with all applicable laws regarding hazardous materials and maintain all required Manufacturer's Safety Data Sheets (MSDS) forms on site in the City.

6.5 During regular business hours, all telephones at Corporation shall be answered by human, not automated, attendants.

Section 7. CORPORATION EMPLOYEES

7.1 All personnel employed by Corporation in the performance of such services, functions and responsibilities as described and contemplated herein for the City shall be and remain Corporation employees (the "Corporation Employees").

7.2 Corporation shall be solely responsible for all compensation benefits, insurance and rights of the Corporation employees during the course of employment with Corporation. Accordingly, the City shall not be called upon to assume any liability for or direct payment of any salaries, wages, contribution to pension funds, insurance premiums or payments, workers compensation benefits under (state statutes) et seq., or any other amenities of employment to any of the Corporation Employees or any other liabilities whatsoever, unless otherwise specifically provided herein.

7.3 In conformance with standards established by City, Corporation shall have and maintain the responsibility for and control of the rendition of the services, the standards of performance, the discipline of the Corporation Employees and other matters incident to the performance of the services, duties and responsibilities as described and contemplated herein.

7.4 In order to perform its obligations hereunder, certain Corporation Employees will be assigned to work full-time for the City (the "Designated Employees"). The Designated Employees shall work for the City full-time and shall perform no work for other Corporation clients. Prior to assigning any Designated Employees to the City, Corporation shall subject each prospective Designated Employee to a full background check, including a driver's license review.

7.5 The Corporation Employees shall wear attire with the logo of the City, when and only when, they are performing services for the City, except as otherwise directed by the City Manager.

7.6 The City Manager shall have the right to require Corporation to transfer any of the Designated Employees out of the City, for any reason or no reason. Other than the Assistant City Manager (which is governed by Section 8 below), Corporation agrees to transfer any of the Designated Employees immediately upon notification by the City Manager. The City Manager shall have the right to prohibit any Corporation Employee that is not a Designated Employee from performing any work for the City, and shall also have the right to limit, in any manner, the work done for the City by and Corporation Employee that is not a Designated Employee.

7.7 Corporation shall have the discretion to transfer or reassign any personnel out of the City for the following reasons:

a. Situations where an employee requests a transfer in order to accept a promotion or special assignment, which has been offered to him or her by Corporation upon his or her special education qualifications or career path;
b. Disciplinary reasons;
c. Failure of an employee to meet Corporation performance standards;
d. At the request of the employee.

In the event Corporation transfers or reassigns any employee for the above stated reasons, Corporation shall provide the City Manager with prompt written notice of such transfer or reassignment and explain the basis of the reassignment. Corporation shall not transfer or reassign any of the Corporation Employees for any other reason unless the City Manager concurs prior to any transfer, which concurrence shall not be unreasonably withheld. Any personnel, transferred or reassigned out of the City, pursuant to this subsection, shall not occur without first filling the vacated position as authorized by the City Manager, which shall not be unreasonably withheld.

Section 8. ASSISTANT CITY MANAGER

8.1 The Assistant City Manager shall, among other duties specified by the City Manager:

a. Act as liaison between the City and Corporation;
b. Attend staff meetings, City Council meetings and any agenda meetings, at which attendance by the Assistant City Manager is deemed necessary by the City Manager. Attend other County and State agency meetings and forums as required by the City Manager;

c. Provide information to City Manager and City Council on all relevant and applicable issues;

d. Assist the City in all relations with other Contractors;

e. Serve as the Acting City Manager, at no additional cost to the City, when so designated by the City Manager.

8.2 In the event of a vacancy in the position of the Assistant City Manager, Corporation agrees to make such selections in good faith and in the best interest of the City. The City Manager shall have the opportunity to interview each of the candidates, and no person may be appointed Assistant City Manager without the City Manager's consent, which may be withheld for any reason or no reason, in City Manager's sole discretion.

8.3 In the event the City Manager becomes dissatisfied with the performance of the Assistant City Manager, the City Manager may, in its sole discretion, provide notification to Corporation. Thereafter, representatives of Corporation and the City Manager shall meet to discuss possible remedies of the problems experienced by the City. Corporation agrees to act in good faith in resolving any problems experienced by the City.

Section 9. CONSIDERATION

9.1 The City shall, on a monthly basis, no later than thirty (30) days following the completion of the month, pay to Corporation, in consideration for the stated services and responsibilities, $1/12^{th}$ of the total amount of yearly compensation for the instant year contained in the Compensation Schedule attached hereto as Exhibit B, including any amendment to said schedule for subsequent years as provided for herein (The "Compensation Amount").

9.2 For each Fiscal Year, beginning in the third year of the contract, the Compensation Amount payable to Corporation under the Terms and Conditions of this Agreement shall be in an amount agreed to by the City Manager and Corporation, and approved by the City Council, provided, however, under no circumstances shall the price increase more than ____ percent (___ %) over the price of the prior year. Corporation shall provide to the City Manager a proposed new Exhibit B each year along with the proposed budget.

9.3 If, during any fiscal year, there is a reduction in the scope of services as directed by the City Manager, the Compensation Amount shall be reduced by an amount agreeable to the City Manager and Corporation, but in no event shall the reduction be an amount less than the actual cost, allocated overhead and profit to Corporation of providing the eliminated service. If the City Manager and Corporation are unable to agree upon an amount, the reduction in the Compensation Amount shall be equal to the actual cost, allocated overhead and profit to Corporation of providing the eliminated service. The Compensation Amount may not be increased in any fiscal year without the approval of the City Council.

9.4 For the fiscal year beginning (Year One) and (Year Two) the annual fee for the services pursuant to this Agreement will be $_ _____________ and $____________________ respectively. For years (Year 3) and beyond, the Compensation Amount shall be an amount as determined by the following formula:

[CPI x (15% x Baseline Compensation Amount which is the current year compensation to be adjusted)] + [ECI x (85% x Baseline Compensation Amount which is the current year compensation to be adjusted)]

CPI = Consumer Price Index for all urban consumers as published by U.S. Department of Labor, Bureau of Labor Statistics in the CPI Detailed Report for the month October of the calendar year presently operating in, (_________) region.
ECI = Compensation for Civilians Workers, Not Seasonally Adjusted (Employment Cost Index) for the third quarter of the calendar year presently operating in as published by U.S. Department of Labor, Bureau of Labor Statistics in the Detailed Report.

Such adjustment formula does not take into consideration significant price increases related to gasoline, power, asphalt, fuel, and other commodities or services related to force majeure events. In the event Corporation can demonstrate that significant regional price increases have occurred, that are outside the reasonable control of Corporation, the City and Corporation will engage in good faith efforts to assess the relative impact on the respective variable to the Compensation Amount.

Subject to the foregoing paragraph regarding significant price increases, in no event shall the total upward adjustment of the Compensation Amount pursuant to this section exceed the sum of nine percent (9%) in any given annual period. Further, the Compensation Amount may not be increased in any fiscal year without the approval of the City Council. In addition, should any upward adjustment of the Compensation Amount be negotiated regarding the Agreement, City shall have a similar right to a proportional adjustment upwards of the amounts regarding Corporation's liability for costs, including but not limited to: (1) liability caps for damages and/or fines, (2) repair and maintenance costs, and (3) furniture, fixture and equipment expenditures under this Agreement, which shall all be set out in writing by way of addendum to this Agreement at the time of agreement upon any revised terms.

Section 10. TERM

This Service Agreement shall remain in full force and effect commencing on January 1, 2009 and shall terminate on December 31, 2009.

Section 11. OPTION TO RENEW

This Agreement shall be automatically renewed for a period of five (5) years terms at the expiration of the initial term, unless the City furnishes Corporation affirmative written notice of its intent not to renew this Agreement not less than thirty (30) days prior to the expiration of this Agreement.

Section 12. TERMINATION

12.1 Corporation may terminate this Service Agreement at its discretion either with or without cause, by giving written notice thereof to City; provided, however, that such termination shall not be effective until the one hundred and eightieth (180th) day after receipt thereof by City.

12.2 City may terminate this Service Agreement in its entirety at its discretion either with or without cause, by giving written notice thereof to Corporation; provided, however, that such termination shall not be effective until the one hundred and eightieth (180th) day after receipt thereof by Corporation. City may also terminate this Service Agreement in its entirety, at its discretion with no advance notice, in the event of a transfer of a controlling interest in Corporation (which shall be defined to mean more than 50% of the ownership interest) to a non-related entity. Corporation shall notify the City Manager immediately upon the transfer of a controlling interest in Corporation.

12.3 City may partially terminate this Service Agreement as to any specific service or services provided by Corporation hereunder by giving at least sixty (60) days advance written notice thereof to Corporation specifying the specific service or services that the City desires Corporation to cease performing. Upon a partial termination, the Compensation Amount shall be reduced pursuant to Section 9.3 of this Agreement.

12.4 In the event of termination by either party, the other party shall render such aid, coordination and cooperation as might be required for an expeditious and efficient termination of service.

Section 13. DEFAULT

13.1 An event of default shall mean a breach of this Agreement. Without limiting the generality of the foregoing and in addition to those instances referred to as a breach, an event of default shall include the following:

a. Corporation has not performed services on a timely basis;
b. Corporation has refused or failed, except in the case for which an extension of time is provided, to supply enough properly skilled Staff personnel;
c. Corporation has failed to obtain the approval of the City where required by this Agreement;
d. Corporation has refused or failed, except in the case for which an extension of time is provided, to provide the Services as defined in this Agreement.

13.2 In the event Corporation fails to comply with the provisions of this Agreement, the City may declare Corporation in default, notify Corporation in writing, and give Corporation fifteen (15) calendar days to cure the default. If Corporation fails to cure the default, compensation will only be for any completed professional services minus any damages pursuant to Section 13.3. In the event payment has been made for such professional services not completed, Corporation shall return these sums to the City within ten (10) days after notice that these sums are due. Nothing in this Article shall limit the City's right to terminate, at any time, pursuant to Sections 11 and 12, its right for damages under Section 13.3, and its right to assign pursuant to Section 38.

13.3 In an Event of Default by Corporation, it shall be liable for all damages resulting from the default.

13.4 The City may take advantage of each and every remedy specifically existing at law or in equity. Each and every remedy shall be in addition to every other remedy specifically given or otherwise existing and may be exercised from time to time as often and in such order as may be deemed expedient by the City. The exercise or the beginning of the exercise of one remedy shall not be deemed to be a waiver of the right to exercise any other remedy. The City's rights and remedies as set forth in this Agreement are not exclusive and are in addition to any other rights and remedies available to the City in law or in equity.

Section 14. TRANSITION

SECTION 14. TRANSITION

14.1 In the event of the full termination for any reason, partial termination or expiration of this Agreement, Corporation and City shall cooperate in good faith in order to effectuate a smooth and harmonious transition from Corporation to City, or to any other person or entity City may designate, and to maintain during such period of transition the same quality services otherwise afforded to the residents of the City pursuant to the terms hereof.

14.2 In the event of the full termination, partial termination or expiration of this Agreement, the City shall have the absolute right to offer employment to any of the Corporation Employees. If, upon termination for any reason other than default of the Corporation, City exercises its option to assume employment of Corporation's employees as contemplated by this Section 14.2, in addition to the Compensation Amount due to Corporation for the completed services, as prorated pursuant to Section 9.5 herein, City shall pay to Corporation as additional compensation the following as compensation to Corporation for expended funds related to employment, training, benefit packages, start-up and transition costs that Corporation would not be able to recoup:

If termination and assumption of Corporation employees occurs in the first year of this Agreement, City shall pay to Corporation the sum of: (1) 35% for staff with salaries above $100,000, and (2) 20% for staff with salaries less than $100,000. For each subsequent renewal period the percentage due for each assumed employee shall be reduced at 1/6 per year such that there is no payment at the end of the Term. The percentage amounts shall be based upon the then current salaries of the respective staff members during the contract year in which the termination takes place.

14.3 In the event of the full termination, partial termination or expiration of this Agreement, and in the further event that the City is unable to provide the same level of services at the time of such termination or expiration, the then pending term of this Agreement may be extended by the City for a period of ninety (90) days or until City is capable, in its sole discretion, of rendering such services, whichever occurs sooner. The remuneration to be paid to Corporation during the transition period shall be based upon actual cost of providing such services during the transition period plus a mutually agreed upon fee, provided, however such fee shall not exceed the Compensation Amount which would be due and owing to the Corporation for the provision of said services pursuant to the terms of this Agreement.

14.4 In the event of the full termination, partial termination, expiration of the term or non-renewal of the term, the City may either accept assignment of Corporations' current leases and/or agreements for the project or City may pay any associated buy-out or termination charges, provided, however, prior to entering into any leases or agreements after the effective date of this Agreement which contain buy-out provisions or termination charges in excess of $1,000.00, Corporation shall submit the terms of the same to the City Manager for approval in writing prior to entering into such lease or agreement. Corporation has provided City with a list of all leases and agreements entered into by Corporation and City hereby approves such.

14.5 The following terms apply to vehicles assets leased by Corporation during the term of this Agreement:

a. Corporation will enter into a lease agreement with ______________________________ for the vehicles required for performance of the services under this Agreement for the City's benefit.

b. Corporation will be responsible for maintaining the required insurance for the leased assets.

c. The Compensation Amount under Section 9 has provided for reimbursement to Corporation for the monthly lease amounts.

d. Under Corporation's lease with ________, after the initial twelve (12) months Corporation has the option to continue to lease the vehicles on a month to month basis; return the vehicle(s) to______; or purchase the vehicle(s). Any time after the initial twelve (12) months, City may request to purchase the vehicle at Corporation's cost plus a transfer fee and applicable taxes, at which point Corporation will exercise its purchase option with

Section 15. INDEMNIFICATION

15.1 Corporation shall indemnify, defend and hold harmless the City, its officers, agents, servants and employees from and against any and all liability, suits, actions, damages, costs, losses and expenses, including attorneys' fees, demands and claims for personal injury, bodily injury, sickness, diseases or death or damage or destruction of tangible property, arising out of any errors, omissions, misconduct or negligent acts, errors, or omissions of Corporation, its officials, agents, employees or subcontractors in the performance of the services of Corporation under this Agreement, whether direct or indirect and from and against any orders, judgments, or decrees which may be entered thereon and from and against all costs, damages of every kind and nature, attorneys' fees, expenses and liabilities incurred in and about the defense of any such claim and investigation thereof.

15.2 Corporation acknowledges that specific consideration has been paid or will be paid under this Agreement for this hold harmless and indemnification provision, and further agrees with the foregoing provisions of indemnity and with the collateral obligation of insuring said indemnity as set forth In Section 16, Insurance.

Section 16. INSURANCE

16.1 Corporation shall not commence work under this contract until Corporation has obtained all insurance required under this paragraph and such insurance has been approved by the City Manager.

16.2 Corporation shall at all times carry professional liability insurance, workers' compensation insurance, comprehensive general liability insurance, and automotive liability insurance with policy limits and deductibles for each coverage at amounts reasonably approved by the City Manager, with such coverages specifying reasonable amounts of per occurrence, single limit, for property damage and bodily injury, including death, except that the dollar amount of workers compensation coverage shall be as provided by (state statutes) et. seq. Corporation shall be responsible for maintaining this professional liability insurance for a minimum of three (3) years from the date of expiration of this Agreement. Upon request of City, Corporation shall make available for inspection copies of any claims filed or made against any policy during the policy term. Corporation shall additionally notify City, in writing, within thirty (30) calendar days, of any claims filed or made against any policy in excess of $5,000 during the policy term.

16.3 Certificates of insurance, reflecting evidence of the required insurance, shall be filed with the City Manager or designee prior to the commencement of the work. Policies shall be issued by companies authorized to do business under the laws of the State of _______, with financial ratings acceptable to the City

Manager. The City shall be named as an additional insured on all insurance policies. Corporation agrees to furnish City with at least thirty (30) days prior written notice of any cancellation of any insurance policy required under this Agreement.

16.4 In the event the insurance certificate provided indicates that the insurance shall terminate and lapse during the period of this contract, then in that event, Corporation shall furnish, at least ten (10) days prior to the expiration of the date of such insurance, a renewed certificate of insurance as proof that equal and like coverage for the balance of the period of the contract and extension hereunder is in effect. Corporation shall not continue to work pursuant to this contract unless all required insurance remains in full force and effect.

16.5 The costs of all policies of insurance required hereunder shall be the obligation of Corporation and the City shall in no way be responsible therefore.

16.6 City shall pay for and maintain its own comprehensive general liability insurance or maintain a self-insuring fund for the term of this Agreement in the amount determined by City to adequately insure the City's liability assumed herein, but in no event shall coverage be less than the amount of statutory waiver of sovereign immunity. In the event such coverage is modified, in any regard, before the expiration date of this Agreement, and unless otherwise agreed, City will provide at least thirty (30) days prior written notice to Corporation.

Section 17. CONFLICTS OF INTEREST/COLLUSION/ CONTINGENT FEES

17.1 Corporation shall not review or perform any services regarding any application made to the City by any client of Corporation, unless the services Corporation performs for such client are unrelated to the City. In such instance, Corporation shall disclose the relationship immediately to the City Manager, who may retain an alternate to Corporation for those services. If the services relate to a fixed fee service, the fees for the alternate to Corporation shall be deducted from the fixed fee paid to Corporation.

17.2 Neither Corporation nor any of its employees shall have or hold any employment or contractual relationship that is antagonistic or incompatible with Corporation's loyal and conscientious exercise of judgment related to its performance under this Agreement.

17.3 Neither Corporation nor any of its officers or employees shall obtain any kickbacks or benefits for itself, themselves or other clients as a result of any City purchases or transactions.

17.4 Corporation shall not collude or enter into any business relationships with other City contract providers regarding City business or matters, without the approval of the City Manager, which may be withheld at the City Manager's sole discretion.

17.5 Corporation warrants that it has not employed or retained any company or person, other than a bona fide employee working solely for Corporation, to solicit or secure this Agreement, and that it has not paid or agreed to pay any person, company, corporation, individual or firm, other than a bona fide employee working solely for Corporation, any fee, commission, percentage, gift, or other consideration contingent upon or resulting from the award or making of this Agreement. For the breach or violation of this provision, the City shall have the right to terminate the Agreement without liability at its discretion, to deduct from the contract price, or otherwise recover the full amount of such fee, commission, percentage, gift or consideration.

Section 18. POLICY OF NON-DISCRIMINATION

Corporation shall not discriminate against any person in its operations, activities or delivery of services under this Agreement. Corporation shall affirmatively comply with all applicable provisions of federal, state and local equal employment laws and shall not engage in or commit any discriminatory practice against any person based on race, age, religion, color, gender, sexual orientation, national origin, marital status, physical or mental disability, political affiliation or any other factor which cannot be lawfully used as a basis for service delivery.

Section 19. DRUG FREE WORKPLACE

Corporation shall maintain a Drug Free Workplace.

Section 20. INDEPENDENT CONTRACTOR

Corporation, for the purposes of this Service Agreement, is and shall remain an independent contractor; not an employee, agent, or servant of the City. Personal services provided by Corporation shall be by employees of Corporation and subject to supervision by Corporation, and not as officers or employees of City. Personnel policies, tax responsibilities, social security and health insurance, employee benefits, and other similar administrative procedures applicable to services rendered under this Agreement shall be those of Corporation.

Section 21. COSTS AND ATTORNEY'S FEES

If the City is required to enforce the terms of this Agreement by court proceedings or otherwise, whether or not formal legal action is required, the Corporation shall pay the attorney's fees and costs of both the City and the Corporation.

Section 22 RIGHTS IN DATA; COPYRIGHTS; DISCLOSURE

22.1 Definition. The term "Data" as used in this Agreement includes written reports, studies, drawings, or other graphic, electronic, chemical or mechanical representation.

22.2 Rights in Data. Drawings, specifications, designs, models, photographs, computer CADD discs, reports, surveys and other data developed or provided in connection with this Agreement shall be the property of City and City shall have the full right to use such data for any official purpose permitted under __ _____ Statutes, including making it available to the general public. Such use shall be without any additional payment to or approval by Corporation. City shall have unrestricted authority to publish, disclose, distribute and otherwise use, in whole or in part, any data developed or prepared under this Agreement.

22.3 Copyrights. No data developed or prepared in whole or in part under this Agreement shall be subject to copyright in the United States of America or other country, except to the extent such copyright protection is available for the City. Corporation shall not include in the data any copyrighted matter unless Corporation obtains the written approval of the City Manager and provides said City Manager with written permission of the copyright owner for Corporation to use such copyrighted matter in the manner provided herein.

22.4 If this Agreement is terminated for any reason prior to completion of the work, the City may, in its discretion, use any design and documents prepared hereunder.

Section 23. COMPLIANCE WITH LAWS; ADVICE OF OTHER PROFESSIONALS

23.1 Corporation shall fully obey and comply with all laws, ordinances and administrative regulations duly made in accordance therewith, which are or shall become applicable to the services performed under the terms of this Agreement.

23.2 Corporation acknowledges that the City is advised by its City Attorney and that, on all legal matters, Corporation shall abide by the advice and direction of the City Attorney in the performance of its duties as they relate to matters of the City.

23.3 Corporation acknowledges that the City is also advised by various other professionals (including, but not limited to, engineers, traffic engineers, planners, building officials, police officers and firefighters), and that, on all matters within their respective expertise, Corporation shall abide by their advice and direction in the performance of its duties as they relate to matters of the City.

Section 24. OWNERSHIP OF WORK PRODUCT DOCUMENTS

24.1 All work product prepared by Corporation for the City shall immediately become the property of the City.

24.2 Corporation understands and agrees that any information, document, report or any other material whatsoever which is given by the City to Corporation or which is otherwise obtained or prepared by Corporation under the terms of this Agreement is and shall at all times remain the property of the City.

Section 25. AUDIT AND INSPECTION RIGHTS

25.1 The City may, at reasonable times, and for a period of up to three (3) years following the date of final performance of Services by Corporation under this Agreement, audit, or cause to be audited, those books and records of Corporation that are related to Corporation's performance under this Agreement. Corporation agrees to maintain all such books and records at its principal place of business for a period of three (3) years after final payment is made under this Agreement. Corporation shall make all necessary books and records available for audit in (county), (state).

25.2 The City may, at reasonable times during the term hereof, inspect Corporation's facilities and perform such inspections, as the City deems reasonably necessary, to determine whether the services required to be provided by Corporation under this Agreement conform to the terms of this Agreement. Corporation shall make available to the City all reasonable facilities and assistance to facilitate the performance of inspections by the City's representatives.

Section 26. WARRANTIES OF CORPORATION

Corporation hereby warrants and represents that at all times during the term of this Agreement it shall maintain in good standing all required licenses, certifications, and permits required under federal, state and local laws necessary to perform the Services.

Section 27. PUBLIC RECORDS

Corporation understands that the public shall have access, at all reasonable times, to all documents and information pertaining to the City, subject to the provision of (state)__ et seq., and agrees to allow access by the City and the public to all documents subject to disclose under applicable law. Corporation's failure or refusal to comply with the provisions of this Section shall result in the immediate termination of this Agreement by the City. Corporation agrees to retain all public records in accordance with the City's records retention and disposal policies, per ______________ ______________Administrative Code.

Section 28. GOVERNING LAW; CONSENT TO JURISDICTION

This Agreement shall be construed in accordance with and governed by the laws of the State of ________. The parties submit to the jurisdiction of any ________ state or federal court in any action or proceeding arising out of, or relating to, this Agreement. Venue of any action to enforce this Agreement shall be in ___________County.

Section 29. HEADINGS

Headings are for the convenience of reference only and shall not be considered in any interpretation of this Agreement.

Section 30. SEVERABILITY

If any provision of this Agreement or the application thereof to any person or situation shall, to any extent, be held invalid or unenforceable, the remainder of this Agreement, and the application of such provisions to persons or situations other than those as to which it shall have been held invalid or unenforceable, shall not be affected thereby, and shall continue in full force and effect, and be enforced to the fullest extent permitted by law.

Section 31. CONFLICT

In the event of a conflict between the terms of this Agreement and any terms or conditions contained in any attached documents, the terms in this Agreement shall prevail.

Section 32. SURVIVAL OF PROVISIONS

Any terms or conditions of this Agreement that require acts beyond the date of its termination shall survive the termination of this Agreement, shall remain in full force and effect unless and until the terms of conditions are completed, and shall be fully enforceable by either party.

Section 33. ENTIRE AGREEMENT

33.1 This Agreement and its attachments constitute the entire agreement between Corporation and City, and all negotiations and oral understandings between the parties are merged herein.

33.2 No modification, amendment or alteration in the terms or conditions of this Agreement shall be effective unless contained in a written document executed with the same formality as this Agreement.

Section 34. WAIVER

The waiver by either party of any failure on the part of the other party to perform in accordance with any of the terms or conditions of this Agreement shall not be construed as a waiver of any future or continuing similar or dissimilar failure.

Section 35. EQUIPMENT APPRAISAL AND TRANSFER

35.1 In the event of full termination, partial termination or expiration of this Agreement, City shall have the option to purchase from Corporation any piece of equipment, directly attributable to or in use by Corporation in the City at the time of such termination or expiration in connection with the services contemplated herein, or, as to a partial termination, in connection with the eliminated services.

35.2 The purchase price for such equipment shall be determined by mutual agreement of the parties as to the fair market value of such equipment.

35.3 Upon the exercise by the City of its option to possess the subject equipment, Corporation shall convey within ten (10) days or upon such other mutually agreed time, all of its rights, title and interest, thereto, to the City by Bill of Sale Absolute or Certificate of Title, as applicable.

Section 36. AUTHORITY TO EXECUTE: NO CONFLICT CREATED

36.1 Corporation by execution hereof does hereby represent to City that Corporation has full power and authority to make and execute this Service Agreement, to the effect that:

a. The making and execution hereof shall create a legal obligation upon Corporation, which shall be legally binding upon Corporation.

b. The same shall be enforceable by the City according and to the extent of the provisions hereof.

36.2 Nothing contained or any obligation on the part of Corporation to be performed hereunder shall in any way be contrary to or in contravention of any policy of insurance or surety bond required of Corporation pursuant to the laws of the State of _______.

36.3 Corporation shall perform this Agreement only under the name of ___________________.

36.4 The City Manager, Mayor and City Clerk, by their respective executions hereof, do each represent to Corporation that they, collectively, have full power and authority to make and execute this Service Agreement on behalf of the City, pursuant to the Resolution of the City Council of the City.

36.5 Nothing herein contained is intended in any way to be contrary to or in contravention of the Charter of the City and the Laws of the State of Georgia, and to the extent such conflict exists; the City and Corporation shall be mutually relieved of any obligations of such conflict.

36.6 In the event of any litigation arising from this Agreement, venue shall be in DeKalb County, _________.

Section 37. NOTICES

Whenever either party desires to give notice to the other, it must be given by written notice, sent by certified United States mail, with return receipt requested, hand delivered or by facsimile transmission with proof of receipt, addressed to the party for whom it is intended, at the place last specified, and the place for giving of notice in compliance with the provisions of this paragraph. Notice shall be deemed given upon receipt by any method of delivery authorized above. For the present, the parties designate the following as the respective places for giving of notice:

For Corporation
For City:

Section 38. ASSIGNABILITY

Corporation shall not assign any of the obligations or benefits imposed hereby or contained herein, without the written consent of the City Council of the City, which consent must be evidenced by a duly passed Resolution. This contract for services is partially and/or fully assignable by the City on sixty (60) days notice to Corporation. Notice of Assignment shall be mailed via U.S. Mail, return receipt requested and any notice required hereunder shall be addressed to the party intended to receive the same at the addresses noted in Section 38. In the event that the City exercises its option to assign this agreement pursuant to this section, the City is not obligated to provide the Notice of Termination identified in Section 12 of this contract. However, Corporation shall coordinate and cooperate with the City as may be required for expeditious and efficient assignment of service pursuant to this article. In addition, Corporation shall transition this contract pursuant to this section in accordance with Section 14 of this Agreement.

Section 39. NEGOTIATION

The parties acknowledge that the terms of this Agreement were jointly negotiated between the parties, that both parties were represented by attorneys and that, in the case of any dispute regarding the terms of this Agreement, the terms should not be construed in favor of or against either party.

Section 40. BINDING EFFECT

This agreement shall inure to the benefit of and be binding upon the respective parties' successors.

SECTION 41. DISPUTES

41.1 To facilitate the timely and effective resolution of any controversy or dispute that may arise under this Service Agreement or out of the performance of this Service Agreement, each party shall appoint one representative to serve on a Management Board. The Management Board will resolve any issues that arise from the Service Agreement that cannot be resolved from the project management level. The party believing there is a controversy or dispute shall put such notice in writing and deliver to the other party. Such demand shall be filed within a reasonable time after the dispute or claim has arisen, but in no event after the applicable statute of limitations for a legal or equitable proceeding would have run. The Management Board shall convene to discuss such notice and shall make a good faith effort to resolve any issues within a period of thirty (30) days of its receipt.

41.2 If a compromise is not negotiated within sixty (60) days of the written notice then in that event the parties shall refer the matter to non-binding mediation. If the parties can not come to an agreement after the non-binding mediation, any claim or counterclaim for less than Two Hundred Thousand Dollars ($200,000) in damages shall be decided by a single arbitrator appointed by the parties for determination as per American Arbitration Association procedures. If the parties are unable to agree on a single arbitrator, each party shall appoint one arbitrator, and the appointed arbitrators shall select a third arbitrator who shall serve as chairperson of the arbitration panel. The third arbitrator selected as chairman shall be a disinterested person of recognized competence. Such arbitration shall be non-binding. The prevailing party shall be entitled to recover its attorney's fees and costs for such arbitration or court proceeding in proportion to the percentage of the recovery. Each party shall pay 50% of the third party costs of arbitration.

41.3 Unless the parties mutually agree otherwise, rules comparable to the Commercial Industry Arbitration Rules of the American Arbitration Association then in effect shall govern the proceedings, provided that failure of the arbitrator(s) to comply with the American Arbitration Association rules shall not invalidate the decision by the arbitrator(s). Notwithstanding Section 28, *Governing Law*, the parties agree this Agreement specifically acknowledge and agree that this contract evidences a "transaction involving commerce" under the Federal Arbitration Act, and that this Agreement to arbitrate shall be governed by the Federal Arbitration Act.

41.4 In those binding arbitration situations, the prevailing party shall be entitled to recover its attorney's fees and costs for such arbitration in proportion to the percentage of the recovery. Each party shall pay 50% of the third party costs of arbitration.

41.5 Should either party seek damages for an amount over $________ ______________, in a claim or counterclaim, either party may file for litigation as per Section 28.

41.6 Unless otherwise agreed in writing, Corporation shall continue to provide services during any dispute resolution proceedings. If Corporation continues to perform, City shall continue to make payments in accordance with this Agreement. During the period, the parties are in dispute resolution proceedings, such Agreement shall be not be deemed to be in default as per Section 13, provided, however, the election to pursue a material breach by virtue of this Section 42 dispute resolution provision shall not constitute a waiver of any breach of the Agreement.

AGREEMENT BY AND BETWEEN CORPORATION AND THE CITY OF ________ FOR CONTRACT SERVICES AS SET FORTH HEREIN.

IN WITNESS WHEREOF, the parties hereto have caused their respective agents to execute this instrument on their behalf, at the times set forth below.

CORPORATION

______________________________ ______________________________

By: DATE

ATTEST

__________________________ __________________________
DATE

CITY OF ___________

__________________________ __________________________

By: DATE
Mayor and Chair

__________________________ __________________________

By: DATE
City Manager

__________________________ __________________________

By: DATE
City Clerk

Approved as to form and legal
Sufficiency subject to execution
by the parties

__________________________ __________________________

By: DATE
City Attorney

CONTRACT BY AND BETWEEN CORPORATION AND

THE CITY OF ___________

INDEX TO EXHIBITS

Exhibit "A"	**Scope of Services**
Exhibit "B"	**Compensation Schedule Year One**
Exhibit "C"	**Compensation Schedule Year Two**

EXHIBIT "A"

SCOPE OF SERVICES

Services include, but are not limited to the following:

1.1 ADMINISTRATIVE SERVICES

Administrative services shall include, but not be limited to the following.

1.1.1 Contract Administration

1.1.1.1 Assist the City Manager in negotiating City contracts, as directed by the City Manager.

1.1.1.2 Advise the City Manager on the status of negotiations as well as contract provisions and their impacts on the City.

1.1.1.3 Make recommendations on contract approval, rejection, amendment, renewal, and cancellation, as directed by the City Manager

1.1.1.4 Provide contract administration and supervision of all contracts, as directed by the City Manager.

1.1.1.5 Ensure ongoing protection of City interests.

1.1.1.6 Ensure compliance with all laws related to bidding, contracting and purchasing as set forth in the State of ___ ___.

1.1.1.7 Assist and coordinate any necessary grant applications and submissions as directed by the City Manager.

1.1.2 **Policy Implementation**

1.1.2.1 Research current and likely future trends impacting the City.

1.1.2.2 Prepare administrative and financial analysis of all available options.

1.1.2.3 Attend all City Council meetings, hearing and agenda meetings, as directed by the City Manager.

1.1.2.4 Assist City Manager with identification of significant policies and analyze their administrative and financial impacts.

1.1.2.5 Prepare plans and procedures to ensure implementation of the City Council policies and directives, as directed by the City Manager.

1.1.2.6 Prepare status reports to advise the City Manager of the progress and results of public policy implementation.

1.1.3 **Daily Communications**

1.1.3.1 Respond to all inquires as directed.

1.1.3.2 Prepare correspondence regarding City affairs for the City Manager and City Clerk, as requested.

1.1.3.3 Ensure compliance with all Open Records and Open Meetings laws as set forth in <u>(state statute)</u> <u>et seq.</u>

1.1.4 **Customer Service**

1.1.4.1 Provide first-tier response to customer inquiries.

1.1.4.2 Establish response protocols and direct customers to the appropriate party.

1.1.5 **Departmental Support**

1.1.5.1 Provide overall administrative support of all City functions and departments.

1.1.6 **Clerking Support**

1.1.6.1 Record and transcribe all City Council meetings, hearing and agenda meetings.

1.1.6.2 Assist City Clerk during Council meetings, take attendance, record motions and votes taken, and swear in witnesses of others presenting testimony to the Council.

1.1.6.3 Assist in the review of documents to be presented to the Council, as directed by the City Manager.

1.1.6.4 Upon City Clerk's absence, authenticate all City documents by appropriate signatures and City Seal.

1.1.6.5 Retain public records and make them available for inspection by the public, in conformance with State Law.

1.1.6.6 Prepare all Council meeting agendas.

1.1.6.7 Publish all appropriate public notices.

1.1.6.8 Serve administrative needs of any and all Boards, Authorities or other entities established by the City for the furtherance of City objectives.

1.1.7 **Records Management**

1.1.7.1 Implement and maintain a custom-designed, state-of-the-art Document Management System to facilitate creating and saving all documents into the system (Word & Excel), then archiving these documents.

1.1.7.2 Improve employee productivity, collaboration, and document security by allowing the users to search for documents by profile information, content, person who created them, or even last person to edit the document. Users may also modify a previously created document for their use while leaving the original document unmodified.

1.1.7.3 Provide sufficient document scanning stations in City Hall so that any and all paper documents such as signed contracts, ordinances, resolutions, and other important City documents may be imported into the Document Management System using the Document Scanning Station.

1.1.7.4 Protect integrity of all public records in accordance with the requirements of State law.

1.1.7.5 Promote sharing of information and collaborative work between all City staff.

1.1.7.6 Provide an application server that will store and manage required data.

1.1.7.7 Provide and maintain access to data to other City contract providers as necessary.

1.1.7.8 Design state-of-the-art storage strategies and systems for all public records. Implement and coordinate the transfer of any and all necessary data, records, or other materials such storage systems anto as necessary for the operation of the City.

1.1.8 **Public Relations**

1.1.8.1 Maintain continuous dialog and communications with City residents with timely updates, as directed by the City Manager.

1.1.8.2 Promote City policy, programs and achievements.

1.1.8.3 Serve as a liaison with residents, civic groups and other governments, as directed by the City Manager.

1.1.8.4 Document important City events for future use in City-developed publications.

1.1.9 **Annual Reports**

1.1.9.1 Develop a graphical and thematic design theme for the Annual Report, for approval by the city Manager.

1.1.9.2 Coordinate with the graphic designers, photographers, editors and others as necessary.

1.1.9.3 Provide effective written and non-written communications to reflect the year's message and inform residents of the City's actions and achievements.

1.1.9.4 Produce, print and deliver the annual reports to City residents.

1.1.10 **City Website**

1.1.10.1 Design and host the City website containing City contact information, statistics, history, departmental and facility description, Council meeting schedule, meeting agendas, agenda packages, minutes, City Codes, notices, and City in pictures and multimedia.

1.1.10.2 Update the site daily to post latest agendas, packages and minutes, notices, etc. and redesign the site annually.

1.1.10.3 Publish City-provided GIS database interface on the website.

1.1.11 **City Newsletter**

1.1.11.1 Provide text, pictures, graphics, maps, exhibits, etc. as necessary for the quarterly newsletter.

1.1.11.2 Coordinate with the publishers to produce a useful, informative, timely and attractive publication.

1.1.11.3 Produce, print and deliver a quality newsletter to all City residents.

1.1.12 **Program Presentation**

1.1.12.1 Publish studies, reports and analysis for staff and public presentation, as directed by the City Manager.

1.1.12.2 Prepare various media presentations of City programs to the staff and general public, as directed by the City Manager.

1.1.13 **Information Technologies and Telephone Systems**

1.1.13.1 Provide, install and maintain state-of-the-art information technology, software and hardware sufficient to efficiently satisfy all City needs.

1.1.13.2 Provide a state-of-the-art domain network to account for handling future growth and technologies.

1.1.13.3 Provide, install, configure and maintain a state-of-the-art server at City Hall and all City offices to improve performance ensure against data loss and minimize potential down time.

1.1.13.4 Provide centralized management of all network resources and a central location for the storage of the City's documents.

1.1.13.5 Ensure data security and integrity with a nightly backup (with offsite storage) and the ability to restore from a central location.

1.1.13.6 Provide, configure and maintain (number)_____ state-of-the-art laptop computers to the members of the City Council (__), City Manager (__), and City Clerk (__).

1.1.13.7 Provide, install, configure and maintain state-of-the-art computer workstations, as needed.

1.1.13.8 Provide digital phones and remote connections for park sites.

1.1.13.9 Maintain software and hardware uniformity and interchangeability among users.

1.1.13.10 Provide, install and maintain sufficient network laser printers to efficiently conduct all City business.

1.1.13.11 Maintain a three-year replacement program for all computers and equipment.

1.1.13.12 Provide, install and maintain state-of-the-art network cabling/data line system for communications, networking and data sharing.

1.1.13.13 Provide, install, configure and maintain servers in support of utility functions.

1.1.13.14 Provide all users with Internet and e-mail connections on a separate server for internal and external communications and common contact lists and scheduling.

1.1.13.15 Archive all e-mails in compliance with State retention requirements.

1.1.13.16 Provide, install and maintain a state-of-the-art telephone system in all City facilities with sufficient lines and features to satisfy all needs of the City.

1.1.14. **Databases – Municipal Management Software**

1.1.14.1 Provide, install, configure and maintain a state-of-the-art database program to manage the City's occupational and business license functions

1.1.14.2 Coordinate the procurement, installation, configuration and maintenance of all databases required of municipalities in the State of ______ by any governmental agencies.

1.1.15 **Court Services**

1.1.15.1 Provide all aspects of court record keeping and reporting as required by law and sound practices including but not limited to maintenance of calendars, recording of sentences and dispositions, coordination with probation services, coordination of collection of fees, fines and surcharges.

1.1.15.2 Provide adequate administrative personnel for Court hearings.

1.1.15.3 Oversee and maintain all systems required for fee, fine and surcharge accounting, reporting and remittance.

1.1.16 **Police**

1.1.16 Provide administrative and clerical assistance in all aspects of police department record keeping and reporting as required by law and sound practices in coordination with City authorities.

1.1.17 **Fire**

1.1.17 Provide administrative and clerical assistance in all aspects of fire department record keeping and reporting as required by law and sound practices in coordination with City authorities.

1.1.18 **Election Support**

1.1.18.1 Coordinate municipal and special elections as required, including but not limited to addressing polling station issues, preparation of ballot questions, or other related issues arising from election matters.

1.1.19 **Solid Waste**

1.1.19.1 Manage and coordinate all aspects of agreements with solid waste providers.

1.2 **FINANCIAL SERVICES**

Financial Services shall include, but not be limited to the following.

1.2.1 **Revenue Collection**

1.2.1.1 Coordinate with local, state and federal agencies charged with collection and disbursement of taxes, assessments, fees, charges and other impositions.

1.2.1.2 Administer the fees, charges and their miscellaneous revenues pertaining to utilities, private enterprises and individuals as they interface with the City programs.

1.2.1.3 Recommend enforcement actions to the City Manager to induce payment in accordance with the City's policies and procedures.

1.2.1.4 Prepare monthly financial reports showing revenues and expenses to date in comparison with budget projections and submit the reports to the City Manager no later than the tenth day of the following month.

1.2.1.5 Maintain a City address list for the Department of Revenue to ensure that the City obtains all shared revenues to which it is entitled.

1.2.2 **Capital Program Administration:**

1.2.2.1 Coordinate with the designated city representatives the capital needs of the City.

1.2.2.2 Obtain financing if necessary and maintain proper fund accounting procedures.

1.2.2.3 Administer and implement capital program financing.

1.2.3 **Investment Services**

1.2.3.1 Recommend investment policies and procedures pursuant to State law.

1.2.3.2 Invest City funds per approved policies.

1.2.3.3 Produce timely investment reports stating the effectiveness of the chosen investment policy.

1.2.4 **Fund Accounting**

1.2.4.1 Establish Fund Accounting System in accordance with Governmental Accounting Standards Board (GASB), the Uniform Accounting System prescribed by Department of Community Affairs and the rules of the State Department of Audits and Accounts.

1.2.4.2 Prepare reports for Department of Community Affairs and State Revenue Department and distributions.

1.2.4.3 Prepare all other financial reports as required by applicable law and accounting standards.

1.2.5 **Accounts payable/receivable**

1.2.5.1 Administer the purchase order system and make timely payment of all invoices.

1.2.5.2 Coordinate tax collection, franchise fees, utility taxes and all other receivables.

1.2.6 **General fixed asset accounting**

1.2.6.1 Account for assets constructed by or donated to the City for maintenance.

1.2.6.2 Inventory City property in accordance with GASB and the State Department of Audits and Accounts.

1.2.7 **Budgeting:**

1.2.7.1 Prepare and submit to the City Manager annual budgets per GASB standards.

1.2.7.2 Liaison with all City departments for annual budget categories.

1.2.7.3 Provide material for and attend all budget meetings, hearing and agenda meetings.

1.2.7.4 Coordinate with other departments and governmental entities as necessary.

1.2.7.5 Present findings in oral, print, multimedia, and web-based forms.

1.2.8 **Forecasting:**

1.2.8.1 Prepare detailed financial forecasts and analysis.

1.2.8.2 I dentify trends and analyze their impact upon City's finances, operations and capital.

1.2.8.3 Develop policy and action recommendations.

1.2.8.4 Coordinate with other departments and governments.

1.2.8.5 Present findings in oral, print, multimedia, and web-based forms.

1.2.9 **Comprehensive Annual Financial Report (CAFR):**

1.2.9.1 Prepare the Annual Financial Report for Units of Local Government, in accordance with Generally Accepted Accounting Principals as defined by the Government Finance Officers Association.

1.2.10 **Risk Management:**

1.2.10.1 Recommend and advise the City Manager of the appropriate amounts and types of insurance and be responsible for procuring all necessary insurance.

1.2.10.2 Process and assist in the investigation of insurance claims, in coordination with the City Attorney.

1.2.10.3 Develop and maintain a risk management claims review procedure, in coordination with the City Manager and City Attorney.

1.2.10.4 Review insurance policies and coverage amounts of City vendors.

1.2.11 **Human Resources:**

1.2.11.1 Ensure proper functioning of payroll, fringe benefit, insurance tax and other City-specific and general law-provided human resources functions.

1.2.11.2 Establish a Code of Conduct for personnel that emphasize the responsibility of the staff to be professional, patient and responsive under all circumstances. The Code should emphasize that rudeness and impoliteness toward any person is unacceptable conduct and will not be tolerated.

1.2.11.3 Establish and implement with all employees an Employee Policies and Procedures Manual, which shall include, but not be limited to, policies and procedures on carrying out duties to the City, consequences of non-compliance to policies, and functions and roles of the employees.

1.2.12 **Purchasing:**

1.2.12.1 Recommend to the City Manager and assist in the implementation of procurement policies and procedures.

1.2.12.2 Assist in selection of vendors.

1.2.12.3 Participate in county and state level purchase plans.

1.2.12.4 Prepare RFP's, as directed by the City Manager.

1.2.12.5 Prepare and process requisitions.

1.2.13 **HIPAA**

1.2.13.1 Ensure that all City systems and procedures meet the requirements of HIPAA.

1.3 **COMMUNITY SERVICES**

1.3.1 **Water Management and Utilities:**

1.3.1.1 Manage and coordinate all aspects of intergovernmental relationship regarding water and sewer issues.

1.3.4 **Animal Control**

1.3.4.1 Provide field staff for the daily maintenance of animal control issues in the City.

2.0 **EMERGENCY 911 SERVICE**

2.1 **Emergency 911 Infrastructure and Staffing**

2.2 Implementing and staff emergency 911 system for the City in accordance with state law and in conjunction with any necessary vendors and local governmental entities.

3.0 **PHYSICAL PLANT REQUIREMENTS**

3.1 **Office, Administrative and Facilities Space**

3.1.1 Provide facilities sufficient for the operations of all departments and functions the City whether or not Corporation is responsible for said operations or function. All space shall meet all minimum (state) requirements, and exhibit a level of finish customary for a local government. Should the City assume any lease, or purchase the property, from the Corporation, the Corporation will be relieved of this obligation. In the event of a lease or purchase of space, the Corporation shall not have rent obligations for any personnel performing duties in behalf of the City.

3.2 **Facilities Maintenance, Repair and Contracts**

3.2.1 Provide personnel to maintain, repair, clean, and keep in good working order all facilities commensurate with local governmental standards all facilities occupied by the City. This provision, however, shall not apply to landscaping maintenance of any City rights-of-way or land.

3.3 **Furniture, Fixtures, Equipment and Supplies**

3.3.1 Provide Furniture, Fixtures, Equipment and Supplies in an amount sufficient for the reasonable operation of all departments and functions the City on the date of acceptance of the proposal, whether or not Corporation is responsible for said operations or function.

4.0 **PURCHASING, PROCUREMENT AND CONTRACTING**

4.1 Corporation shall meet or exceed all laws and requirements regarding purchasing, and procurement as set forth by the State of _________Corporation shall also meet or exceed all laws and requirements regarding the same as set forth by the State of _______, regarding any contracting required in the course of fulfilling the duties under this Agreement.

CONTRACT BY AND BETWEEN CORPORATION AND THE CITY OF ___________.

EXHIBIT "B" ADENDUM

Compensation Schedule YEAR ONE

<u>RESERVED</u>

CONTRACT BY AND BETWEEN CORPORATION AND THE CITY OF ___________________.

EXHIBIT "C" ADDENDUM

Compensation Schedule YEAR TWO

RESERVED

APPENDIX C - SAMPLE CONTRACT

(Note – this sample is derived from the contracts of a new city with a Public/Private partnership. It is an excellent guide for a new city. It should be a good guide for an existing city that plans to convert to a P/P/P. There are certain elements such as the transfer of data from the county etc. that will need to be deleted. Additional elements will most likely be needed to deal with such issues as the transfer of personnel from the city to the company, and with the specific needs of the issuing city that differ from the model.

While the contract is similar to the proposed contract in the RFP, it reflects changes that resulted from contract negotiation.

AGREEMENT BY AND BETWEEN

____

AND

____

FOR PROVISION OF

ADMINISTRATIVE, FINANCIAL COMMUNITY SERVICES, MOTOR VEHICLE, STAFFING, AND PURCHASING, PROCUREMENT AND CONTRACTING SERVICES

AND SERVICES FOR
PUBLIC WORKS, TRANSPORTATION, STREETS, RIGHT-OF-WAY, FACILITIES, PARKS AND RECREATION, CAPITAL IMPROVEMENTS, PLANNING AND ZONING, INSPECTIONS, CODE ENFORCEMENT, PERMITTING

THIS AGREEMENT is made and entered into this _____ day of ___ _______, 200__, by and between the CITY OF _______________, a (STATE) municipal corporation, (the "City"), and (COMPANY) Inc., a (STATE) corporation. ("Corporation").

WHEREAS, the City is desirous of maintaining a level of competent professional and economically feasible contract administrative, finance and community services in conjunction and harmony with its fiscal policies of sound, economical management, and

WHEREAS, Corporation has agreed to render to the City a continuing level of professional contract services and the City is desirous of contracting for such services upon the terms and conditions hereinafter set forth, and

WHEREAS, Corporation is licensed to do business within the state of ______ as a foreign corporation, and

WHEREAS the City is desirous of providing these daily services to its constituents through a contractual relationship with Corporation,

WHEREAS the (ISSUING BODY) for the City of _____ ____, an entity created pursuant to (STATUTE), followed a specific procedure, issued a request for proposals, and the proposals were reviewed by representatives of the City and were made available to the members of the public at large,

WHEREAS the City has the power to contract,

WHEREAS the City will have on-hand funds to pay for all obligations incurred hereunder,

NOW THEREFORE, in consideration of the sums hereinafter set forth and for other good and valuable considerations, the receipt and legal sufficiency of which are hereby acknowledged, it is hereby agreed as follows:

SECTION 1. PRIOR AGREEMENTS

As of the effective date hereof, all prior agreements between the City and Corporation are terminated and replaced by the terms hereof.

SECTION 2. GENERAL SERVICES

2.1 Corporation shall provide to City for the term hereinafter set forth, as the same may be extended in accordance with the provisions hereof, competent services, within and throughout the corporate limits of City to the extent and in the manner hereinafter described.

2.2 The City hereby engages Corporation to provide, and Corporation hereby agrees to provide, all of the services described herein and in the "Scope of Services," attached hereto as Exhibit A and incorporated herein by reference.

2.3 The parties recognize that this Agreement is intended to provide flexibility to the City in order to meet its evolving challenges. The Corporation reserves the right to reasonably allocate resources for the performance of services under this agreement for Administrative, Financial Community Services, Motor Vehicle, Staffing, And Purchasing, Procurement And Contracting Services Public Works, Transportation, Streets, Right-Of-Way, Facilities, Parks And Recreation, Capital Improvements, Planning And Zoning, Inspections, Code Enforcement, and Permitting, per the priorities agreed-to with the City Manager so long as such allocations do not adversely affect the City regarding either (1) cost of services under this Agreement, or (2) service quality to the public. Staff additions as agreed upon between the parties resulting from new services outside the Scope of Services in this contract, will be considered a change to this Agreement.

2.4 Corporation agrees to provide City all services and personnel necessary to fulfill the obligations of Corporation under this contract; provided, however, that to the extent that the City must cooperate and/or perform services in conjunction with a third party, excluding Corporation's second tier subcontractors which shall be defined as any individual or entity retained, employed, affiliated, or engaged by or under contract with Corporation to undertake any services performed hereunder, should the third party fail to fulfill their obligations or duties, any additional services performed or costs reasonably incurred by the Corporation in conjunction with compensating for the failure of the third party to fulfill its obligations shall be handled as a change to this Agreement as per Section 9.1.1.

2.5 Except as otherwise hereinafter specifically set forth, such professional services shall encompass all those duties and functions of the type coming within the jurisdiction of and customarily rendered by municipal departments (other than those provided by other contract providers) in accordance with the Charter of the City, and the Statutes of the State of ____.

2.6 Corporation shall, at all times, foster and maintain harmonious relationships with the members of the City Council, all employees of the City, all employees of the City's contract services providers and all City's residents, and shall represent the City in the best light possible.

2.7 All communications to the Mayor, City Council, and press, unless otherwise authorized, shall be through the City Manager. All mass communications to residents shall be reviewed and approved by the City Manager prior to printing and dissemination.

2.8 The President or Senior Executive Officer of Corporation shall be available to meet with the City Manager at City Hall on an annual basis, date to be determined by mutual agreement, and at any other times at the request of the City Manager after reasonable notice has been provided to President or Senior Executive Officer of Corporation.

SECTION 3. FINANCIAL SERVICES

3.1 Corporation shall follow the procedures established by the City Manager for withdrawal, transfer and disbursement of City funds.

3.2 Corporation shall maintain all financial records in accordance with all applicable laws and guidelines for municipal accounting, including ______________________ standards, and shall produce and deliver to the City Manager any and all financial information and reports requested by the City Manager.

3.3 Corporation shall ensure that the City complies with all requirements regarding audits, and shall assist the City in procuring an independent auditor with experience in governmental auditing in compliance with all applicable laws and procedures.

3.4 All investments shall be made pursuant to any and all investment policies approved by the City Council in accordance with (STATE) Statutes.

3.5 Corporation shall prepare and follow risk management policies and procedures, as adopted by the City Council.

3.6 Corporation shall take advantage of all available discounts on purchases and invoices for City purchases, unless, based upon best cash management practices, a more beneficial payment structure is available to the City.

3.7 Corporation shall promptly pay all City bills in accordance with (STATE) law and sound business practices.

3.8 Corporation shall assist the City in finding and applying for various grants and in fulfilling all obligations that accompany such grants.

3.9 On or before the fifteenth day of each month, Corporation shall prepare and deliver to the City Manager a monthly financial statement for the prior month.

3.10 On or before October 1 of every year, Corporation shall prepare and deliver to the City Manager an annual inventory of all City owned tangible personal property and equipment in accordance with all applicable rules and standards.

SECTION 4. ADDITIONAL SERVICES

4.1 Corporation shall provide to the City, upon the request of the City Manager and the availability of resources, such additional services as may from time to time be needed at the discretion of the City.

4.2 The cost of such additional services shall be borne by the City and shall be payable in such amounts and in such a manner as may be determined by mutual agreement, upon each occurrence in accordance with Section 9.1.1.

4.3 Corporation may provide management of capital improvements and engineering services (provided, however, Corporation acknowledges that it is responsible for certain engineering services encompassed in the Scope of Agreements for Admistrative, Financial Community Services, Motor Vehicles, staffing, Public Works, Transportation, Streets, Right-Of-Way, Facilities, Parks And Recreation, Capital Improvements, Planning And Zoning, Inspections, Code Enforcement, Permitting, Purchasing, Procurement, and Contracting Services executed contemporaneously herewith) as set out in Sections ______ of the Scope of Services attached hereto as Exhibit A. Both Parties agree that Corporation's duties under this Agreement are limited to the coordination for capital improvement programs and procurement and program management for small projects (i.e., estimated procurement contract value of under $50,000 although final decision will be based upon the complexity of said project), unless otherwise agreed upon between the Parties. Corporation's duties do not include the program management of the large or complex (those projects outside of the above definition of small projects) which would be outside the Scope of Services herein and, accordingly, handled through an additional services authorization and change to the Agreement as per Section 9.1.1 of this Agreement. Subject to all other requirements contained herein, the parties agree that if requested to conduct program management of the operations of a capital improvement project, Corporation may provide for such services to be completed by either Corporation, an affiliate of Corporation, or second tier subcontractor.

4.4 MAINTENANCE. REPAIR AND CAPITAL IMPROVEMENTS

1. Corporation shall provide for ordinary maintenance of City assets and infrastructure in the course of its duties under

this Agreement as per Exhibit A, Scope of Services. Such ordinary maintenance shall be performed to the extent of the capabilities of the project staff during normal business hours. For the purposes of this Agreement, the definition of ordinary maintenance shall be: the routine/repetitive activities required for operational continuity, safety, and performance of City assets or infrastructure.

2. Corporation shall provide for repair of City assets and infrastructure in the course of its duties under this Agreement as per Exhibits A and B, Scope of Services. For the purposes of this Agreement, the definition of repair shall be: the cost of non-routine/non-repetitive activities required for operational continuity, safety, and performance generally resulting from the failure or to avert a failure of the equipment, vehicle, roadway, or facility or some component thereof. The parties agree that such repair work shall be limited $50,000 annually unless otherwise specified in the Scope of Services or unless and in the event Corporation is responsible for the needed repairs through its failure to perform routine maintenance or because of any intentional acts of the Corporation's employees. The parties further agree that Corporation is authorized pursuant to this agreement to immediately perform emergency repair services which may fall outside of the Scope of Services hereto to address unforeseen issues of safety and welfare which may arise, provided, however, Corporation and shall notify the City Manager of the existence of, and the scope of, any such emergency repair as soon as feasible based upon the circumstances, but in no event later than twenty-four (24) hours of receipt of notification of such emergency repairs.

3. A capital improvement is defined as, any work or materials applied to an existing asset that restores that asset or infrastructure to a "like new" condition and/or improves the performance and/or reliability levels of the asset beyond the capabilities of the original installation or performs a duty or service that was not previously provided. The Corporation's duties under this Agreement do not encompass payment for capital improvements to assets of the City unless so agreed to between the parties.

SECTION 5. HOURS OF OPERATION

5.1 Corporation shall maintain for the purposes of City business, fully staffed business hours equal to, but not less than, the City's business hours of 8:00 a.m. to 5:00 p.m. and shall reasonably provide appropriate staff to perform the after hours requirements associated with court services, clerking support, public relations, and election support to fulfill the performance of the services as per Exhibit A, Monday through Friday, with the exception of the following holidays:

New Year's Day
President's Day
Memorial Day
Independence Day
Labor Day
Veteran's Day
Thanksgiving Day
Day After Thanksgiving Day
Christmas

5.2 For all City related matters, Corporation shall use the address of (CITY) City Hall, including both incoming and outgoing mail.

SECTION 6. EQUIPMENT AND LABOR

6.1 Corporation shall furnish to and maintain, as per Section 3 of the Exhibit A, for the benefit of the City, without additional cost, all necessary labor, supervision, equipment (including motor vehicles excluding, however, any specialized service related emergency vehicles such as Police and/or Fire Emergency Vehicles) necessary and proper for the purpose of performing the services, duties and responsibilities set forth and contemplated herein and as necessary to maintain the level of service to be rendered hereunder. In the event of emergencies or natural disasters, Corporation shall, immediately and on and on-going basis, supply its usual and customary personnel to ensure continuing operation of all services provided by Corporation and to satisfy all County, State and Federal administrative and emergency requirements.

6.2 All City owned equipment shall be used only for City purposes in performance of this Agreement, and shall not be used for any purely corporate, non-governmental Corporation business or personal purposes.

6.3 All City owned vehicles and equipment utilized by Corporation employees shall be maintained in strict accordance with manufacturer's recommended maintenance, and Corporation shall keep full records of all maintenance. All City vehicles shall be kept clean, free of damages and in safe operating condition. All City vehicles shall be used in strict conformance with the Vehicle Use Policy attached hereto as Exhibit __.

6.4 Corporation shall comply with all OSHA and other applicable federal and state statutes, regulations and standards for work place safety. Corporation shall comply with all applicable laws regarding hazardous materials and maintain all required Manufacturer's Safety Data Sheets (MSDS) forms on site in the City.

6.5 During regular business hours, all telephones at Corporation shall be answered by human, not automated, attendants

SECTION 7. CORPORATION EMPLOYEES

7.1 All personnel employed by Corporation in the performance of such services, functions and responsibilities as described and contemplated herein for the City shall be and remain Corporation employees (the "Corporation Employees").

7.2 Corporation shall be solely responsible for all compensation benefits, insurance and rights of the Corporation employees during the course of or arising or accruing as a result of any employment, whether past or present, with Corporation, as well as all legal costs including attorney's fees incurred in the defense of any conflict or legal action resulting from such employment or related to the corporate amenities of such employment. Accordingly City shall not be called upon to assume any liability for or direct payment of any salaries, wages, contribution to pension funds, insurance premiums or payments, workers compensation benefits under (STATUTE) et seq., or any other amenities of employment to any of the Corporation Employees or any other liabilities whatsoever, unless otherwise specifically provided herein.

7.3 In conformance with standards established by City for achieving an acceptable level of customer service and delivery of municipal services to the City residents and constituents consistent with reasonable municipal management practices as compared with municipalities of similar size in the State of _____, Corporation shall have and maintain the responsibility for and control of the rendition of the services, the standards of performance, the discipline of the Corporation Employees and other matters incident to the performance of the services, duties and responsibilities as described and contemplated herein.

7.4 In order to perform its obligations hereunder, certain Corporation Employees will be assigned to work full-time for the City (the "Designated Employees"). Prior to assigning any Designated Employees to the City, Corporation shall subject each prospective Designated Employee to a full background check, including a driver's license review. Corporation retains the ability to discipline such Designated Employees as per Corporation's established guidelines, including termination.

7.5 The Corporation Employees shall wear attire with the logo of the City when, and only when, they are performing services for the City, except as otherwise directed by the City Manager.

7.6 The City Manager shall have the right utilizing an objective standard based upon job performance to require Corporation to transfer any of the Designated Employees out of the City or to a different position. Corporation agrees to transfer any of the Designated Employees immediately upon notification by the City Manager. Utilizing an objective standard based upon job performance, the City Manager shall have the right to prohibit any Corporation Employee that is not a Designated Employee from performing any work for the City, and shall also have the right to limit, in any manner, the work done for the City by any Corporation Employee that is not a Designated Employee.

7.7 Corporation shall have the discretion to transfer or reassign any personnel out of the City for the following reasons:

a. Situations where an employee requests a transfer in order to accept a promotion or special assignment, which has been offered to him or her by Corporation upon his or her special education qualifications or career path;

b. Disciplinary reasons;

c. Failure of an employee to meet Corporation performance standards;

d. At the request of the employee.

In the event Corporation transfers or reassigns any employee for the above stated reasons, Corporation shall provide the City Manager with prompt written notice of such transfer or reassignment and explain the basis of the reassignment. Corporation shall not transfer or reassign any of the Corporation Employees for any other reasons unless the City Manager concurs prior to any transfer, which concurrence shall not be unreasonably withheld. Any personnel, transferred or reassigned out of the City, pursuant to this subsection, shall not occur without first filling the vacated position with a Corporation employee approved and authorized by the City Manager, which approval and authorization shall not be unreasonably withheld.

SECTION 8. ASSISTANT CITY MANAGER AND PROGRAM DIRECTOR

8.1 The Program Director assisted by the Assistant City Manager shall, among other duties specified by the City Manager:

a. Act as liaison between the City and Corporation;

b. Attend staff meetings, City Council meetings and any agenda meetings, at which attendance by the Program Director and Assistant City Manager is deemed necessary by the City Manager. Attend other County and State agency meetings and forums as required by the

City Manager;

c. Provide information to City Manager and City Council on all issues relevant and applicable to the City, its officials, its constituents or to its status as a municipal corporation;

d. Assist the City in all relations with other Contractors;

e. When so directed by the City Manager, carry out such other duties and responsibilities as are necessary to fulfill services under Exhibit A, but that are not inconsistent with Corporation's obligations under this Agreement, nor expand Corporation's obligations under this Agreement.

8.2 In the event of a vacancy in the position of the Program Director and/or Assistant City Manager, Corporation agrees to make such selections in good faith and in the best interest of the City. The City Manager shall have the opportunity to interview each of the candidates, and no person may be appointed Program Director or Assistant City Manager without the City Manager's consent which may be withheld for any or no reason, in City Manager's sole discretion.

8.3 In the event the City Manager becomes dissatisfied with the performance of the Program Director or Assistant City Manager, utilizing an objective standard based upon job performance, the City Manager may, in its sole discretion, provide notification to Corporation. Thereafter, representatives of Corporation and the City Manager shall meet to discuss possible remedies of the problems experienced by the City. Corporation agrees to act in good faith in resolving any problems experienced by the City, including if necessary the removal of _____ as Assistant City Manager or _______ as Program Director.

SECTION 9. COMPENSATION

9.1 The City shall pay to Corporation as compensation for services performed under this Agreement a fixed price of $________

for the first year of this Agreement ("Compensation Amount"). One-twelfth (1/12) of the Compensation Amount shall invoiced by the first of the month in which services are to be performed and the invoice shall be due thirty (30) days from receipt. The City shall budget an additional fifteen percent (15%) of the annual Compensation Amount for new services not defined in Exhibits A and B, Scope of Services. Access to these funds will be controlled by the City and authorized via the defined Change Order process outlined in Section 9.2 of this Service Agreement. **The Compensation Amount does not include Sales, Use or other taxes. Such applicable taxes will be added to the monthly invoice.** Such Compensation Amount shall be adjusted on an annual basis as per Section 9.4, to take effect on January 1st of the new calendar year in which Corporation is performing services. Corporation shall provide to City on a monthly basis the breakdown of monthly price per overall service in a format to be agreed upon between the parties.

9.2 The City from time-to-time may request the Corporation to perform services which are not included in Exhibit A, Scope of Services ("Change Order"). Upon request by the City, the Corporation will, within a reasonable time period (generally within 5 working days) provide to the City a price for the Change Order service(s) in writing. The estimate will be provided to the City for review and approval. If approved by the City in writing, the Corporation will proceed with the Change Order services. Unless otherwise stated in the estimate, the Corporation will invoice the City on the next billing cycle after completion of Change Order service(s). If the Change Order service request generates an on-going new service or will result in an on-going new service under the Scope of Services, the Corporation will include the associated adjustment for the Change Order to the monthly Compensation Amount invoice for City consideration.

9.3 City shall pay interest at an annual rate equal to ________ Banks, prime rate plus one and one-half percent (1-1/2%) (said amount of interest not to exceed any limitation provided by law) on payments not paid and received within thirty (30) calendar days from date of receipt by the City of Corporation's monthly invoice, such interest being calculated from the due date of the payment, so long as said delay is not caused by Corporation. City shall pay all undisputed amounts according to the terms of this Agreement. If City disputes any invoices issued, City shall notify Corporation in writing within five (5) days of receipt of invoice detailing out the invoice charge disputed and reasons why. Corporation shall respond within five (5) days to such notification. If such issue is not resolved within fifteen (15) days after notification, such issue shall be handled as per Section 42. Valid disputes on invoices shall not accrue interest until the date of resolution, and applicable interest, if any, shall be calculated from the date of resolution of the dispute.

9.4 For the fiscal year beginning January 1, 2009, the annual fee for the services pursuant to this Agreement will be $_________. For years Fiscal Year 2010 and beyond, the Compensation Amount shall be an amount as determined by the following formula:

[CPI x (15% x Baseline Compensation Amount which is the current year compensation to be adjusted)] + [ECI x (85% x Baseline Compensation Amount which is the current year compensation to be adjusted)]

CPI = Consumer Price Index for all urban consumers as published by U.S. Department of Labor, Bureau of Labor Statistics in the <u>CPI Detailed Report</u> for the month October of the calendar year presently operating in, (______ region, State)

ECI = Compensation for Civilians Workers, Not Seasonally Adjusted (Employment Cost Index) for the third quarter of the calendar year presently operating in as published by U.S. Department of Labor, Bureau of Labor Statistics in the <u>Detailed Report</u>.

Such adjustment formula does not take into consideration significant price increases related to gasoline, power, asphalt, fuel, and other commodities or services related to force majeure events. In the event Corporation can demonstrate that significant regional price increases have occurred, that are outside the reasonable control of Corporation, the City and Corporation will engage in good faith efforts to assess the relative impact on the respective variable to the Compensation Amount.

Subject to the foregoing paragraph regarding significant price increases, in no event shall the total upward adjustment of the Compensation Amount pursuant to this section exceed the sum of nine percent (9%) in any given annual period. Further, the Compensation Amount may not be increased in any fiscal year without the approval of the City Council. In addition, should any upward adjustment of the Compensation Amount be negotiated regarding the Agreement, City shall have a similar right to a proportional adjustment upwards of the amounts regarding Corporation's liability for costs, including but not limited to: (1) liability caps for damages and/or fines, (2) repair and maintenance costs, and (3) furniture, fixture and equipment expenditures under this Agreement, which shall all be set out in writing by way of addendum to this Agreement at the time of agreement upon any revised terms.

9.5 If, during any fiscal year, there is a reduction in the scope of services not related to default by Corporation as per Section 13, the Compensation Amount shall be reduced by an amount agreeable to the City Manager and Corporation, but in no event shall the reduced Compensation Amount be an amount less than the actual cost of said services, and the allocated overhead and profit for such services. If the City elects not to assume performance of the reduced or eliminated services as contemplated herein, and therefore the equipment, materials and staff procured or hired by Corporation for the provision to the City of said reduced services results in expense to the Corporation, Corporation may recover those expenses caused by such unassumed services including any demobilization costs, unamortized costs incurred by Corporation, and any applicable termination charges assessed by vendors or suppliers retained by Corporation to provide the eliminated service. If the City Manager and Corporation are unable to agree upon an amount, the reduced Compensation Amount shall be equal to the actual cost, allocated overhead and profit, less any allowed offsets as set forth in this Section.

9.6 The parties may agree to modify the baseline compensation amount for Fiscal Year 20__, provided, however, should

Corporation seek to modify such baseline amount such request must be made in writing directed to the City Manager, setting forth all costs and justifications for such modification no less than six (6) months prior to the termination date under the Agreement. Any modification of the baseline compensation amount shall be subject to approval of the City Council.

SECTION 10. TERM

As per (STATUTE), this Service Agreement is effective January 1, 20__, and shall be effective for one year terms ending at the close of each calendar year. This Service Agreement shall be automatically renewed as per Section 11.

SECTION 11. OPTION TO RENEW

As per (STATUTE), this Agreement shall be automatically renewed for a period of five (5) one (1) year terms at the expiration of the initial term, upon the mutual agreement between the Parties, unless either party furnishes the other party written notice of its intent not to renew this Agreement not less than one hundred twenty (120) days prior to the expiration of this Agreement.

SECTION 12. TERMINATION

12.1 Corporation may terminate this Service Agreement at its discretion either with or without cause, by giving written notice thereof to City; provided, however, that such termination shall not be effective until the one hundred and eightieth (180th) day after receipt thereof by City.

12.2 City may terminate this Service Agreement in its entirety at its discretion either with or without cause, by giving written notice thereof to Corporation; provided, however, that such termination shall not be effective until the one hundred and eightieth (180th) day after receipt thereof by Corporation. City may also terminate this Service Agreement in its entirety, at its discretion with no advance notice, in the event of a vote by the Board of Directors, officers or employees to transfer of a controlling interest in Corporation (which shall be defined to mean more than 50% of the ownership interest) to a non-related entity. Corporation shall notify the City Manager immediately in the event of such a vote to so transfer of a controlling interest in Corporation.

12.3 City may partially terminate this Service Agreement as to any specific service or services provided by Corporation hereunder by giving at least sixty (60) days advance written notice thereof to Corporation specifying the specific service or services that the City desires Corporation to cease performing. Upon a partial termination, the Compensation Amount shall be reduced pursuant to Section 9.5 of this Agreement.

12.4 In the event of termination by either party, the other party Shall render such aid, coordination and cooperation as might be required for an expeditious and efficient termination of service.

In the event of termination by City for reasons other than default as per Section 13, and if the City elects not to assume performance of some or all of the reduced services Corporation may recover costs as set forth in Section 9.5 of this Agreement.

12.5 This Service Agreement is contingent upon sufficient appropriation and authorization being made annually by the City Council, at least one hundred and twenty (120) days prior to renewal period, for the performance of the services provided in this contract. If sufficient appropriations and authorizations are not so made, this Contract shall terminate pursuant to the terms of this Section 12 upon written notice being given by the City to Corporation.

SECTION 13. DEFAULT

13.1 An event of default shall mean a material breach of this Agreement. If situations arise which are not considered a material breach, such issues shall be resolved as per Section 42. Without limiting the generality of the foregoing and in addition to those instances referred to as a breach, an event of default shall include the following:

a. Corporation has not performed services as per this Agreement;

b. Corporation has refused or failed, except in the case for which an extension of time is provided, to supply properly skilled Staff personnel;

c. Corporation has failed to obtain the approval of the City where required by this Agreement;

d. Corporation has refused or failed, except in the case for which an extension of time is provided, to provide the Services as defined in this Agreement.

e. The failure, refusal or other default by the City in its duty: (1) to pay the amount required to be paid to the Corporation under this Agreement within 30 days following the due date for such payment; or (2) to to perform any other material obligation under this Agreement (unless such default is excused by a Force Majeure and to the extent provided herein)

f. Any representation or warranty of either party hereunder that was false or inaccurate in any material respect when made, and which materially and adversely affects the legality of this Agreement or the ability of either party to carry out its obligations hereunder.

13.2 In the event either Party fails to comply with the provisions of this Agreement, the other Party may: (1) declare the Party in default, notify defaulting party in writing, and give defaulting party fifteen (15) calendar days from receipt of notice to make substantial efforts towards curing the default. If defaulting party fails to make substantial efforts towards curing such default within fifteen (15) calendar days, such Agreement shall be terminated as per Section 12.1 and any compensation due and owing to Corporation shall be paid by City; or (2) such party may exercise such provisions under Section 42 regarding the alleged breach without waiving or being estopped from subsequently pursuing the breach as a matter of law. If Corporation is the defaulting party, the compensation to Corporation through termination shall be the prorated Compensation Amount for any completed professional services minus any damages assessed pursuant to Section 13.3. Upon termination City shall begin transition efforts and Corporation shall assist such transition, provided, however, City shall be liable for the reasonable costs for transition efforts as demonstrated by the Corporation. In the event payment has been made for professional services not completed, Corporation shall return these sums to the City within ten (10) days after receipt of notice that these sums are due. Nothing in this Article shall limit the either Party's right to terminate, at any time, pursuant to Sections 11 and 12, its right for damages under Section 13.3, and its right to assign pursuant to Section 38.

13.3 In an Event of Default by either Party, it shall be liable for all damages resulting from the default.

13.4 Subject to the dispute provisions contained in Section 42 of this Agreement, either Party may take advantage of each and every remedy specifically existing at law or in equity. Each and every remedy shall be in addition to every other remedy specifically given or otherwise existing and may be exercised from time to time as often and in such order as may be deemed expedient by the Party. The exercise or the beginning of the exercise of one remedy shall not be deemed to be a waiver of the right to exercise any other remedy. The Parties' rights and remedies as set forth in this Agreement are not exclusive and are in addition to any other rights and remedies available to either Party in law or in equity.

SECTION 14. TRANSITION

14.1 In the event of the full termination for any reason, partial termination or expiration of this Agreement, Corporation and City shall cooperate in good faith in order to effectuate a smooth and harmonious transition from Corporation to City, or to any other person or entity City may designate, and to maintain during such period of transition the same quality services otherwise afforded to the residents of the City pursuant to the terms hereof.

14.2 In the event of the full termination, partial termination or expiration of this Agreement, the City shall have the absolute right to offer employment to any of the Corporation Employees. If, upon termination for any reason other than default of the Corporation, City exercises its option to assume employment of Corporation's employees as contemplated by this Section 14.2, in addition to the Compensation Amount due to Corporation for the completed services, as prorated pursuant to Section 9.5 herein, City shall pay to Corporation as additional compensation the following as compensation to Corporation for expended funds related to employment, training, benefit packages, start-up and transition costs that Corporation would not be able to recoup:

If termination and assumption of Corporation employees occurs in the first year of this Agreement, City shall pay to Corporation the sum of: (1) 35% for staff with salaries above $100,000, and (2) 20% for staff with salaries less than $100,000. For each subsequent renewal period the percentage due for each assumed employee shall be reduced at 1/6 per year such that there is no payment at the end of the Term. The percentage amounts shall be based upon the then current salaries of the respective staff members during the contract year in which the termination takes place.

14.3 In the event of the full termination, partial termination or expiration of this Agreement, and in the further event that the City is unable to provide the same level of services at the time of such termination or expiration, the then pending term of this Agreement may be extended by the City for a period of ninety (90) days or until City is capable, in its sole discretion, of rendering such services, whichever occurs sooner. The remuneration to be paid to Corporation during the transition period shall be based upon actual cost of providing such services during the transition period plus a mutually agreed upon fee, provided, however such fee shall not exceed the Compensation Amount which would be due and owing to the Corporation for the provision of said services pursuant to the terms of this Agreement.

14.4 In the event of the full termination, partial termination, expiration of the term or non-renewal of the term, the City may either accept assignment of Corporations' current leases and/or agreements for the project or City may pay any associated buy-out or termination charges, provided, however, prior to entering into any leases or agreements after the effective date of this Agreement which contain buy-out provisions or termination charges in excess of $1,000.00, Corporation shall submit the terms of the same to the City Manager for approval in writing prior to entering into such lease or agreement. Corporation has provided City with a list of all leases and agreements entered into by Corporation and City hereby approves such.

14.5 The following terms apply to vehicles assets leased by Corporation during the term of this Agreement:

a. Corporation will enter into a lease agreement with __________ Inc. for the vehicles required for performance of the services under this Agreement for the City's benefit.

b. Corporation will be responsible for maintaining the required insurance for the leased assets.

c. The Compensation Amount under Section 9 has provided for reimbursement to Corporation for the monthly lease amounts.

d. Under Corporation's lease with ___, after the initial twelve (12) months Corporation has the option to continue to lease the vehicles on a month to month basis; return the vehicle(s) to ___; or purchase the vehicle(s). Any time after the initial twelve (12) months, City may request to purchase the vehicle at Corporation's cost plus a transfer fee and applicable taxes, at which point Corporation will exercise its purchase option with ___.

SECTION 15. INDEMNIFICATION

15.1 Corporation shall indemnify, defend and hold harmless the City, its officers, agents, servants and employees from and against any and all liability, suits, actions, damages, costs, losses and expenses, including attorneys' fees, demands and claims for personal injury, bodily injury, sickness, diseases or death or damage or destruction of tangible property, to the proportionate extent arising out of any errors, omissions, willful misconduct or negligent acts of Corporation, its officials, agents, employees or subcontractors in the performance of the services of Corporation under this Agreement, from and against any orders, judgments, or decrees which may be entered thereon and from and against all costs, damages of every kind and nature, attorneys' fees, expenses and liabilities incurred in and about the defense of any such claim and investigation thereof. Corporation's indemnification, however, shall be limited to the actual amount of any liability of City and not encompass any sums for which City is exempt based upon (STATE) municipal immunity Statutes.

15.2 Corporation acknowledges that specific consideration has been paid or will be paid under this Agreement for this hold harmless and indemnification provision, and further agrees with the foregoing provisions of indemnity and with the collateral obligation of insuring said indemnity as set forth In Section 16, Insurance.

15.3 To the extent allowable by (STATE) law, City shall indemnify, defend and hold harmless the Corporation, its officers, agents, employees, and subcontractors from and against any and all liability, suits, actions, damages, costs, losses and expenses, including attorneys' fees, demands and claims for personal injury, bodily injury, sickness, diseases or death or damage or destruction of tangible property, to the proportionate extent arising out of any errors, omissions, willful misconduct or negligent acts of City, its officials, agents, servants, or subcontractors in the performance by the City of its obligations under this Agreement, whether from and against any orders, judgments, or decrees which may be entered thereon and from and against all costs, damages of every kind and nature, attorneys' fees, expenses and liabilities incurred in and about the defense of any such claim and investigation thereof.

15.4 In disputes between City and Corporation, in no event shall either party, its subcontractors or their officers or employees be liable to the other party for any special, indirect or consequential damages, whether such liability arises in breach of contract or warranty, tort including negligence, strict or statutory liability, or any other cause of action, provided, however, such limitation does not include any liability for which Corporation is obligated to indemnify City based upon special, indirect or consequential damages suffered by any third-parties.

15.5 In compensation for benefits conveyed to the City by this Agreement, the parties agree that Corporation's liability to the City will, in the aggregate, not exceed $3,500,000 per term of this Agreement. This provision takes precedence over all conflicting provisions of this Agreement except the Severability provision of Section 30. This limitation of liability will apply to all claims brought by the City against the Corporation, whether Corporation's liability to the City arises under breach of contract or warranty; tort, including negligence, strict liability, statutory liability; or any other cause of action, and shall include Corporation's officers, affiliated corporations, employees, and subcontractors. This subsection does not apply to claims for indemnification by the City against Corporation.

15.6 In compensation for benefits conveyed to the City by this Agreement, the parties agrees that Corporation shall be liable for fines or civil penalties to a maximum aggregate of One Hundred Fifty Thousand Dollars ($150,000) per year, which may be imposed by any federal or state department or regulatory agency that are a result of Corporation's negligent operation. City will assist Corporation to contest any such fines in administrative proceedings and/or in court prior to any payment by Corporation. Corporation shall pay the costs of contesting any such fines. Corporation shall not be liable for fines or civil penalties that result from violations that occurred prior to the effective date of this Agreement or for the effects of prior violations by the City that have contributed to the assessment of any fine or civil penalty caused by Corporation's negligent operations.

15.7 City and Corporation shall perform a condition assessment of the assets and infrastructure within sixty (60) days after the execution of this Agreement to establish the existing condition of the assets and infrastructure of the City. The City shall be responsible for the costs, claims, liabilities and expenses related to the condition of the assets up to the assessment determination. Following the date of assessment, Corporation is responsible for maintaining the assets as per this Section 4.4.1 of this Agreement.

SECTION 16. INSURANCE

16.1 Corporation shall not commence work under this contract or continue performance of the services unless and until Corporation has obtained all insurance required under this Section 16 as per the following:

16.1.1 Corporation shall provide the following insurances throughout the term of the Agreement, and shall provide to City Certificates of Insurance demonstrating compliance with this provision:

16.1.1.1 Statutory Worker's Compensation and Employers Liability Insurance as required by the State of______. Such workers compensation coverage shall be as provided by (STATUTE) et. Seq

16.1.1.2 Comprehensive Automobile and Vehicle Liability Insurance with 5 Million Dollars ($5,000,000) combined single limits, covering claims for injuries to members of the public and/or damages to property of others arising from the use of Corporation owned or leased motor vehicles, including onsite and offsite operations.

16.1.1.3 Commercial General Liability Insurance with limits of 5 Million Dollars ($5,000,000) per occurrence and in the aggregate, covering claims for injuries to members of the public or damages to property of others arising out of any covered acts of the Corporation undertaken to provide services for the City as required in this Agreement or omission of Corporation or any of its employees, or subcontractors.

16.1.1.4 Professional Liability Insurance with limits of 5 Million Dollars ($5,000,000) per occurrence and in the aggregate.

16.1.1.5 Excess Liability Insurance with limits of 45 Million Dollars ($45,000,000).

1. City shall warrant that the following insurances are carried throughout the term of the Agreement, and shall provide Corporation with Certificates of Insurance to demonstrate compliance with this provision:

1. Property Damage Insurance for all property including City supplied vehicles and equipment for the full fair market value of such property.

2. Liability Insurance for all motor vehicles and equipment provided by City and operated by Corporation under this Agreement.

2. City and Corporation will insure that any and all policies of insurance procured hereunder shall provide for a waiver of subrogation against the other, and each party waives any claim against the other arising in contract or in tort which are covered by their respective insurance hereunder.

16.3 Corporation shall be responsible for maintaining this professional liability insurance for a minimum of two (2) years from the date of expiration of this Agreement. Upon request of City, Corporation shall make available for inspection copies of any claims filed or made against any policy during the policy term. Corporation shall additionally notify City, in writing, within thirty (30) calendar days, of any claims filed or made as it relates to the scope of services provided under this Agreement against any policy in excess of $25,000 during the policy term.

16.4 Certificates of insurance, reflecting evidence of the required insurance, shall be filed with the City Manager or designee prior to the commencement of the work. Policies shall be issued by companies authorized to do business under the laws of the State of _______, with financial ratings acceptable to the City Manager. The City shall be named as an additional insured on allowable polices obtained regarding services under this Agreement, including but not limited to the Commercial General Liability and Comprehensive Auto Liability insurance policies. Corporation agrees to furnish City with at least thirty (30) days prior written notice of any cancellation of any insurance policy required under this Agreement.

16.5 In the event the insurance certificate provided indicates that the insurance shall terminate and lapse during the period of this contract, then in that event, Corporation shall furnish, fifteen (15) days after expiration of such insurance, a renewed certificate of insurance as proof that equal and like coverage for the balance of the period of the contract and extension hereunder is in effect. Corporation shall not continue work pursuant to this Agreement unless all required insurance remains in full force and effect.

16.6 The costs of all policies of insurance required hereunder shall be the obligation of Corporation and the City shall in no way be responsible therefore.

16.7 City shall pay for and maintain its own comprehensive general liability insurance or maintain a self-insuring fund for the term of this Agreement in the amount determined by City to adequately insure the City's liability assumed herein, but in no event shall coverage be less than the amount of statutory waiver of sovereign immunity. In the event such coverage is modified, in any regard, before the expiration date of this Agreement, and unless otherwise agreed, City will provide at least thirty (30) days prior written notice to Corporation.

16.8 Corporation shall supply a Performance Bond on an annual basis to City in the amount of $500,000 or 10% of the Compensation Amount (whichever is less) to be supplied to City within thirty (30) days of execution of this Agreement.

SECTION 17 CONFLICTS OF INTEREST /COLLUSION/CONTINGENT FEES

17.1 Corporation shall not review or perform any services regarding any application made to the City by any client of Corporation, unless the services Corporation performs for such client are unrelated to the City. In such instance, Corporation shall disclose the relationship immediately to the City Manager, who may retain an alternate contractor or service provider to Corporation for those services the performance of which by the Corporation would create a perceived or real conflict of interest. If the services relate to a fixed fee service, the fees for the alternate to Corporation shall be deducted from the fixed fee paid to Corporation.

17.2 Neither Corporation nor any of its officers or employees shall have or hold any employment or contractual relationship that is antagonistic or incompatible with Corporation's loyal and conscientious exercise of judgment related to its performance under this Agreement.

17.3 Neither Corporation nor any of its directors, officers or employees shall obtain any kickbacks or benefits for itself, themselves or other clients as a result of any City purchases or transactions.

17.4 Corporation shall not collude with other City contract providers regarding City business or matters. Corporation shall not enter into any business relationships with other City contract providers regarding City business or matters, without the approval of the City Manager, which approval may be withheld at the City Manager's sole discretion.

17.5 Corporation warrants that it has not employed or retained any company or person, other than a bona fide employee working solely for Corporation, to solicit or secure this Agreement, and that it has not paid or agreed to pay any person, company, corporation, individual or firm, other than a bona fide employee working solely for Corporation, any fee, commission, percentage, gift, or other consideration contingent upon or resulting from the award or making of this Agreement. Provided however, this provision does not encompass Corporation's ability to have hired or engaged consultants to assist in preparation of the proposal and delivery of the services hereunder. For the breach or violation of this provision, the City shall have the right to terminate the Agreement without liability at its discretion, to deduct from the contract price, or otherwise recover the full amount of such fee, commission, percentage, gift or consideration.

SECTION 18. POLICY OF NON-DISCRIMINATION
Corporation shall not discriminate against any person in its operations, activities or delivery of services under this Agreement. Corporation shall affirmatively comply with all applicable provisions of federal, state and local equal employment laws and shall not engage in or commit any discriminatory practice against any person based on race, age, religion, color, gender, sexual orientation, national origin, marital status, physical or mental disability, political affiliation or any other factor which cannot be lawfully used as a basis for the provision or denial of service delivery.

SECTION 19. DRUG FREE WORKPLACE
Corporation shall maintain a Drug Free Workplace.

SECTION 20. INDEPENDENT CONTRACTOR
Corporation, for the purposes of this Service Agreement, is and shall remain an independent contractor; not an employee, agent, or servant of the City. Personal services provided by Corporation shall be by employees of Corporation and subject to supervision by Corporation, and not as officers or employees of City. Personnel policies, tax responsibilities, social security and health insurance, employee benefits, and other similar administrative procedures applicable to services rendered under this Agreement shall be those of Corporation.

SECTION 21. COSTS AND ATTORNEY'S FEES
If the either party is required to enforce the terms of this Agreement by court proceedings or otherwise due to breach of contract, whether or

not formal legal action is required, the prevailing party shall recover its attorney's fees and costs incurred due to such.

SECTION 22 RIGHTS IN DATA; COPYRIGHTS; DISCLOSURE

22.1 Definition. The term "Data" as used in this Agreement includes written reports, studies, drawings, or other graphic, electronic, chemical or mechanical representation.

22.2 Rights in Data. Drawings, specifications, designs, models, photographs, computer CADD discs, reports, surveys, software, and other data developed or provided in connection with this Agreement (excluding company proprietary documents and software) shall be the property of City and City shall have the full right to use such data for any official purpose permitted under Georgia Statutes, including making it available to the general public. Such use shall be without any additional payment to or approval by Corporation. City shall have unrestricted authority to publish, disclose, distribute and otherwise use, in whole or in part, any data developed or prepared as per this Section 22.2. All software purchased by the Corporation on behalf of City shall be licensed appropriately under the name of the City. Corporation shall disclose to City Manager any anticipated proprietary documents or software before utilization under this Agreement and shall obtain City Manager approval prior to usage. To the extent the Corporation deems it necessary and with the consent of the City Manager; the Corporation may designate any additional software or proprietary information as confidential, a trade secret, or other reason under Georgia law that exempts the information from disclosure.

22.3 Copyrights. No data developed or prepared in whole or in part under this Agreement shall be subject to copyright in the United States of America or other country, except to the extent such copyright protection is available for the City. Corporation shall not include in the data any copyrighted matter unless Corporation obtains the written approval of the City Manager and provides said City Manager with written permission of the copyright owner for Corporation to use such copyrighted matter in the manner provided herein.

22.4 If this Agreement is terminated for any reason prior to completion of the work, the City may, in its discretion, use any design and documents prepared hereunder.

SECTION 23. COMPLIANCE WITH LAWS; ADVICE OF OTHER PROFESSIONALS

23.1 Corporation shall fully obey and comply with all laws, ordinances and administrative regulations duly made in accordance therewith, which are or shall become applicable to the services performed under the terms of this Agreement. Any changes in costs to perform services or comply with such laws, ordinances or administrative regulations or ability of Corporation to perform services due to change in applicable laws, ordinances, governing permits, or administrative regulations after effective date of this Agreement shall entitle Corporation to modification of this Agreement as per Section 9.2

23.2 Corporation acknowledges that the City is advised by its City Attorney and that, on all legal matters, Corporation shall abide by the advice and direction of the City Attorney in the performance of its duties as they relate to matters of the City, provided, however that should compliance with such direction require an increase in the scope of services under this Agreement, such increase shall be handled as per Section 9.2 hereof. Provided, however, in no case shall the Corporation be required to abide by the advice and direction of the City Attorney in the event that such advice would cause the Corporation to violate any of its obligations under this Agreement.

23.3 Corporation acknowledges that the City is also advised by various other professionals (including, but not limited to, engineers, traffic engineers, planners, building officials, police officers and firefighters), and that, on all matters within their respective expertise, subject to the approval of the City Manager, Corporation shall abide by their advice and direction in the performance of its duties as they relate to matters of the City, as long as such advice doesn't increase the scope of services or cost under Agreement. If such direction does increase the scope of services pursuant to this Agreement, it shall be handled as per Section 9.1.1.

SECTION 24. OWNERSHIP OF WORK PRODUCT DOCUMENTS

24.1 All work product prepared by Corporation exclusively for the City shall immediately become the property of the City, excluding other company proprietary documents and software as disclosed pursuant to Section 22.2.

24.2 Corporation understands and agrees that any information, document, report or any other material whatsoever which is given by the City to Corporation or which is otherwise obtained or prepared by Corporation exclusively for City under the terms of this Agreement is and shall at all times remain the property of the City.

SECTION 25. AUDIT AND INSPECTION RIGHTS

25.1 The City may, at reasonable times, and for a period of up to three (3) years period of up three (3) years following the date of final performance of Services by Corporation under this Agreement, audit, or cause to be audited, those books and records of the Corporation that are related to the Corporation's performance under this Agreement, excluding all financial records unless related to direct cost reimbursable expenses or other matters contemplated herein, including but not limited to buy-out provisions, unless a court of competent jurisdiction orders disclosure of such information. Corporation agrees to maintain all such books and records at its principal place of business for a period of three (3) years after final payment is made under this Agreement. Corporation shall make all necessary books and records available for audit in _____ County, (STATE).

25.2 The City may, at reasonable times during the term hereof, inspect Corporation's facilities and perform such inspections and process reviews, as the City deems reasonably necessary, to determine whether the services required to be provided by Corporation under this Agreement conform to the terms of this Agreement. Corporation shall make available to the City all reasonable facilities and assistance to facilitate the performance of inspections by the City's representatives.

SECTION 26. WARRANTIES OF CORPORATION

Corporation hereby warrants and represents that at all times during the term of this Agreement it shall maintain in good standing all required licenses, certifications, and permits required under federal, state and local laws necessary to perform the Services.

SECTION 27. PUBLIC RECORDS

Corporation understands that the public shall have access, at all reasonable times, to all documents and information pertaining to the City, subject to the provision of (STATUTE) et seq., and agrees to allow access by the City and the public to all documents subject to disclosure under applicable law. Corporation's willful failure or refusal to comply with the provisions of this Section shall result in the immediate termination of this Agreement by the City. Corporation agrees to retain all public records in accordance with the City's records retention and disposal policies, (STATUTE) et. seq., and the (STATE) Administrative Code.

SECTION 28. GOVERNING LAW; CONSENT TO JURISDICTION

This Agreement shall be construed in accordance with and governed by the laws of the State of_______. Subject to the arbitration requirements of Section 42, and when federal jurisdiction is permitted, the parties submit to the jurisdiction of federal court in any action or proceeding arising out of, or relating to, this Agreement. Venue of any action to enforce this Agreement shall be in _________________ Federal Court.

SECTION 29. HEADINGS

Headings are for the convenience of reference only and shall not be considered in any interpretation of this Agreement.

SECTION 30. SEVERABILITY

If any provision or subsection of any provision of this Agreement or the application thereof to any person or situation shall, to any extent, be held invalid or unenforceable, the remainder of this Agreement including the general provision of any invalid or unenforceable subsection of a provision, and the application of such provisions to persons or situations other than those as to which it shall have been held invalid or unenforceable, shall not be affected thereby, and shall continue in full force and effect, and be enforced to the fullest extent permitted by law.

SECTION 31. CONFLICT

In the event of a conflict between the terms of this Agreement and any terms or conditions contained in any attached documents, the terms in this Agreement shall prevail.

SECTION 32. SURVIVAL OF PROVISIONS

Any terms or conditions of this Agreement that require acts beyond the date of its termination shall survive the termination of this Agreement, shall remain in full force and effect unless and until the terms of conditions are completed shall be fully enforceable by either party.

SECTION 33. ENTIRE AGREEMENT

33.1 This Agreement and its attachments constitute the entire agreement between Corporation and City, and all negotiations and oral understandings between the parties are merged herein.

33.2 No modification, amendment or alteration in the terms or conditions of this Agreement shall be effective unless contained in a written document executed with the same formality as this Agreement.

SECTION 34. WAIVER

The waiver by either party of any failure on the part of the other party to perform in accordance with any of the terms or conditions of this Agreement shall not be construed as a waiver of any future or continuing similar or dissimilar failure.

SECTION 35. EQUIPMENT APPRAISAL AND TRANSFER

35.1 In the event of full termination, partial termination or expiration of this Agreement, City shall have the option to purchase from Corporation any piece of equipment belonging to the Corporation or purchased by the Corporation to provide the services outlined herein. The City shall also pay any unamortized costs incurred by Corporation at the time of such termination or expiration which are directly attributable to the purchase or use of such equipment..

35.2 The purchase price for such equipment shall be determined by mutual agreement of the parties as to the fair market value of such equipment.

35.3 Upon the exercise by the City of its option to possess the subject equipment and upon payment by City, Corporation shall convey within ten (10) days or upon such other mutually agreed time, all of its rights, title and interest, thereto, to the City by Bill of Sale Absolute or Certificate of Title, as applicable.

SECTION 36. AUTHORITY TO EXECUTE: NO CONFLICT CREATED

36.1 Corporation by execution hereof does hereby represent to City that Corporation has full power and authority to make and execute this Service Agreement, to the effect that:

a. The making and execution hereof shall create a legal obligation upon Corporation, which shall be legally binding upon Corporation.

b. The same shall be enforceable by the City according and to the extent of the provisions hereof.

36.2 Nothing contained or any obligation on the part of Corporation to be performed hereunder shall in any way be contrary to or in contravention of any policy of insurance or surety bond required of Corporation pursuant to the laws of the State of Georgia.

36.3 Corporation shall perform this Agreement under the name of (COMPANY), Inc., provided, however that (COMPANY), Inc. may perform services under this Agreement through any wholly owned affiliates of (COMPANY) and if so, such affiliates shall be bound by the terms and conditions of this Agreement to the same extent as if they had been a signatory hereof. It shall be the duty of Corporation to insure: (1) that any affiliates who conduct business for the City pursuant to this Agreement have executed all documents necessary to be legally bound to the City regarding said business; and (2) that any affiliates who conduct business for the City pursuant to this Agreement are in full compliance with the terms hereof.

36.4 The City Manager, Mayor and City Clerk, by their respective executions hereof, do each represent to Corporation that they, collectively, have full power and authority to make and execute this Service Agreement on behalf of the City, pursuant to the Resolution of the City Council of the City.

36.5 Nothing herein contained is intended in any way to be contrary to or in contravention of the Charter of the City and the Laws of the State of _____, and to the extent such conflict exists; the City and Corporation shall be mutually relieved of any obligations of such conflict.

SECTION 37. NOTICES

Whenever either party desires to give notice to the other, it must be given by written notice, sent by certified United States mail, with return receipt requested, hand delivered or by facsimile transmission with proof of receipt, addressed to the party for whom it is intended, at the place last specified, and the place for giving of notice in compliance with the provisions of this paragraph. Notice shall be deemed given upon receipt by any method of delivery authorized above. For the present, the parties designate the following as the respective places for giving of notice:

For Corporation: (COMPANY)
(ADDRESS)
(FAX)

For City: (NEED TO FILL IN)

SECTION 38. ASSIGNABILITY

Either Party shall not assign any of the obligations or benefits imposed hereby or contained herein, without the written consent of the other Party. Such consent on behalf of the City Council of the City must be evidenced by a duly passed Resolution. Notice of Assignment shall be mailed via U.S. Mail, return receipt requested and any notice required hereunder shall be addressed to the party intended to receive the same at the addresses noted in Section 37. In the event that the City exercises its option to assign this agreement pursuant to this section, the City is not obligated to provide the Notice of Termination identified in Section 12 of this contract. However, Corporation shall coordinate and cooperate with the City as may be required for expeditious and efficient assignment of service pursuant to this article. In addition, Corporation shall transition this contract pursuant to this section in accordance with Section 14 of this Agreement.

SECTION 39. FORCE MAJEURE

Neither party shall be liable for damages, delays, or failure to perform its obligations under this Agreement if performance is made impractical, abnormally difficult, or abnormally costly, as a result of any unforeseen occurrence, including but not limited to fire, flood, strike, acts of God, failure of a third party to cooperate in providing services other than Corporation's second tier subcontractors as such term is defined in paragraph 2.4 of this Agreement, or other occurrences, beyond its reasonable control. The party invoking this Force Majeure clause shall notify the other party immediately by verbal communication and in writing of the nature and extent of the contingency within ten (10) working days after its occurrence, and shall take reasonable measures to mitigate any impact of Force Majeure. If the Force Majuere event shall impact schedule or increases the costs incurred by Corporation (excluding those scope of services already anticipated and detailed out in Exhibits A and B), such items shall be handled as per Section 9.1.1.

SECTION 40. NEGOTIATION

The parties acknowledge that the terms of this Agreement were jointly negotiated between the parties, that both parties were represented by attorneys and that, in the case of any dispute regarding the terms of this Agreement, the terms should not be construed in favor of or against either party.

SECTION 41. BINDING EFFECT

This agreement shall inure to the benefit of and be binding upon the respective parties' successors.

SECTION 42. DISPUTES

42.1 To facilitate the timely and effective resolution of any controversy or dispute that may arise under this Service Agreement or out of the performance of this Service Agreement, each party shall appoint one representative to serve on a Management Board. The Management Board will resolve any issues that arise from the Service Agreement that cannot be resolved from the project management level. The party believing there is a controversy or dispute shall put such notice in writing and deliver to the other party. Such demand shall be filed within a reasonable time after the dispute or claim has arisen, but in no event after the applicable statute of limitations for a legal or equitable proceeding would have run. The Management Board shall convene to discuss such notice and shall make a good faith effort to resolve any issues within a period of thirty (30) days of its receipt.

42.2 If a compromise is not negotiated within sixty (60) days of the written notice then in that event the parties shall refer the matter to non-binding mediation. If the parties can not come to an agreement after the non-binding mediation, any claim or counterclaim for less than Two Hundred Thousand Dollars ($200,000) in damages shall be decided by a single arbitrator appointed by the parties for determination as per American Arbitration Association procedures. If the parties are unable to agree on a single arbitrator, each party shall appoint one arbitrator, and the appointed arbitrators shall select a third arbitrator who shall serve as chairperson of the arbitration panel. The third arbitrator selected as chairman shall be a disinterested person of recognized competence. Such arbitration shall be non-binding. The prevailing party shall be entitled to recover its attorney's fees and costs for such arbitration or court proceeding in proportion to the percentage of the recovery. Each party shall pay 50% of the third party costs of arbitration.

42.3 Unless the parties mutually agree otherwise, rules comparable to the Commercial Industry Arbitration Rules of the American Arbitration Association then in effect shall govern the proceedings, provided that failure of the arbitrator(s) to comply with the American Arbitration Association rules shall not invalidate the decision by the arbitrator(s). Notwithstanding Section 28, *Governing Law*, the parties agree this Agreement specifically acknowledge and agree that this contract evidences a "transaction involving commerce" under the Federal Arbitration Act, and that this Agreement to arbitrate shall be governed by the Federal Arbitration Act.

42.4 In those binding arbitration situations, the prevailing party shall be entitled to recover its attorney's fees and costs for such arbitration in proportion to the percentage of the recovery. Each party shall pay 50% of the third party costs of arbitration.

42.5 Should either party seek damages for an amount over Two Hundred Thousand Dollars ($200,000), in a claim or counterclaim, either party may file for litigation as per Section 28.

42.6 Unless otherwise agreed in writing, Corporation shall continue to provide services during any dispute resolution proceedings. If Corporation continues to perform, City shall continue to make payments in accordance with this Agreement. During the period, the parties are in dispute resolution proceedings, such Agreement shall be not be deemed to be in default as per Section 13, provided, however, the election to pursue a material breach by virtue of this Section 42 dispute resolution provision shall not constitute a waiver of any breach of the Agreement.

AGREEMENT BY AND BETWEEN CORPORATION AND THE CITY OF ____________FOR CONTRACT SERVICES AS SET FORTH HEREIN.

IN WITNESS WHEREOF, the parties hereto have caused their respective agents to execute this instrument on their behalf, at the times set forth below.

_________ INCORPORATED

________________________ ________________________

By: DATE

ATTEST

________________________ ________________________

DATE

CITY OF _________

________________________ ________________________

By: DATE
Mayor and Chair

________________________ ________________________

By: DATE
City Manager

________________________ ________________________

By: DATE
City Clerk
Approved as to form and legal
Sufficiency subject to execution

by the parties

_______________________	_______________________
By:	DATE
City Attorney	

APPENDIX C

EXHIBIT A

SCOPE OF SERVICES

Services described in this Exhibit A will be delivered in a manner that is consistent with reasonable municipal management practices as compared with municipalities of similar size in the State of _______.

The Corporation will provide sufficient staff, including contractor and subcontractor personnel, to provide the services described in this Exhibit A. It is recognized that the project staffing may fluctuate due to seasonal or other conditions to meet the service demands. It is envisioned that the average annual staffing levels will be approximately ________ full-time equivalent (FTE) positions to deliver the intended services consistent with reasonable municipal management practices as compared with municipalities of similar size in the State of ______. If there are modifications to the scope of service that require significant additional staffing levels, such changes will be handled as per Section 9.1.1 of the Agreement. As discussed in the contract, the corporation reserves the right to rearrange such positions as appropriate to address capacity and capability issues for the services under this agreement. Per Section 2.3 of this Agreement, the Corporation has the ability to reallocate resources.

The Corporation has provided references to FTEs in this scope of services to establish a level of effort consistent with reasonable municipal management practices. The corporation shall allocate resources among the scopes of services in this document.

Unless otherwise noted, the Corporation is not responsible for providing security services.

The services to be provided are described in the following sections.

1.1 ADMINISTRATIVE SERVICES

Administrative services shall include the following:

1.1.1 Contract Administration

1.1.1.1 Assist in negotiating City contracts, as directed by the City Manager. The City Manager and/or Mayor shall approve final contracts and execute and bind the City to such agreements.

1.1.1.2 Advise the City Manager on the status of negotiations, as well as contract provisions and their impacts on the City.

1.1.1.3 Make recommendations on contract approval, rejection, amendment, renewal, and cancellation, as directed by the City Manager.

1.1.1.4 Provide contract administration and supervision of contracts and agreements, as directed by the City Manager.. Such tasks shall include, but not be limited to, monitoring contract amendments, obtaining applicable insurance certificates, and monitoring applicable progress.

1.1.1.5 Work with the City Manager to plan and implement processes for the ongoing protection of the City's interests.

1.1.1.6 Recommend and implement policies and procedures to provide for compliance with laws related to bidding, contracting, and purchasing as set forth in the State of ______, by examining the applicable laws and developing procedures for bidding, contracting, and procurement processes.

1.1.1.7 Assist and coordinate necessary grant applications and submissions as directed by the City Manager.

1.1.2 Policy Implementation

1.1.2.1 Research current and likely future trends impacting the City as identified and agreed upon with the City Manager.

1.1.2.2 Prepare administrative and financial analyses related to policy decisions being considered by the City and provide recommendations of available options.

1.1.2.3 Attend City Council meetings, hearings, and agenda meetings as directed by the City Manager.

1.1.2.4 Assist the City Manager with the identification of significant policies and analyze their administrative and financial impacts.

1.1.2.5 Assist the City in the preparation of plans and procedures to implement City Council policies and directives successfully, as directed by the City Manager.

1.1.2.6 Prepare regular monthly status reports and, as required, special reports to advise the City Manager of the progress and results of public policy implementation.

1.1.2.7 This scope does not include support associated with litigation activity, including but not limited performance as expert witnesses, outside of work performance parameters for the respective employee.

1.1.3 Daily Communications

1.1.3.1 Respond and/or coordinate responses to inquires in a timely fashion and in accordance with the established communications plan and policies approved by the City.

1.1.3.2 In accordance with established communications plans and policies, prepare correspondence regarding City affairs as directed and approved by the City Manager and the City Clerk.

1.1.3.3 Assist the City with administrative compliance with Open Records and Open Meetings laws as set forth in the Official Code of (STATE) Annotated Sections ________ et seq.

1.1.3.4 Corporation shall provide nominal and routine assistance to input information into character generation for cable broadcast, as approved by City Manager.

1.1.3.5 This scope of services for communications does not include Public Television broadcast or Web-cast of City events or meetings.

1.1.4 Customer Service

1.1.4.1 Provide staff as opposed to voice mail during business hours as the first point of contact for incoming calls to the City. The initial first year staffing compliment will include a level of effort consistent with ____ dedicated FTEs and _____ backup FTEs to support this function. The backup FTEs will be drawn from other administrative functions as required. After business hours, provide answering service equipped with emergency contact information as needed.

1.1.4.2 Develop and implement response protocols and direct customers to the appropriate party.

1.1.5 Departmental Support

1.1.5.1 Provide administrative clerical support staff at a level of effort consistent with _____FTEs to assist City functions and departments in their respective operations, by doing such tasks as answering the phone, greeting customers, filing, and other miscellaneous clerical tasks.

1.1.6 Clerking Support

Staffing at a level of effort consistent with _____FTE'sShall complete the following:

1.1.6.1 Record and transcribe City Council meetings, hearings and agenda meetings.

1.1.6.2Assist the City Clerk during City Council meetings, take attendance, record motions, record votes taken, and swear in witnesses of others presenting testimony to the Council.

1.1.6.3 Assist in the review of documents to be presented to the City Council, as directed by the City Manager.

1.1.6.4 Upon the City Clerk's absence, authenticate City documents by appropriate signatures and City Seal.

1.1.6.5 Retain public records and make them available for inspection by the public in conformance with Georgia Law.

1.1.6.6 Under the direction of the City Clerk prepare City Council meeting agendas.

1.1.6.7 Under the direction of the City Clerk publish appropriate public notices.

1.1.6.8 Serve the administrative needs of Boards, Authorities, or other entities established by the City for the furtherance of

City objectives that can be reasonably supported by staffing at a level of effort consistent with _____ FTEs.

1.1.6.9 Scope does not include costs to codify City Codes.

1.1.7 Records Management

1.1.7.1 At contract inception, start developing and implementing processes and procedures for manual records management in accordance with State law to facilitate creating, saving, and archiving Microsoft Word® and Excel® documents. These processes and procedures will be transitioned to a commercially available Document Management System that is leading industry technology at the time of installation. Implementation of the Document Management System will be initiated after the implementation of the computerized financial application system is complete. The estimated completion date for the implementation of the Document Management System is on or around ________________ ______.

1.1.7.2 Facilitate employee productivity, collaboration, and document security by allowing the users to search for documents by profile information, content, person who created the document, or last person to edit the document. Users may modify a previously created document for their use if they leave the original document unmodified.

1.1.7.3 Provide up to three (3) Document Scanning Stations in City Hall so that paper documents such as signed contracts, ordinances, resolutions, and other important City documents may be imported into the Document Management System using a Document Scanning Station. Documents that will be scanned will be 8-1/2" x 11" (letter), 8-1/2" x 14" (legal), and 11" x 17".

1.1.7.4 Protect the completeness of public records in accordance with the requirements of State law by storing backups of electronic files off site on a server and hard copy documents at City Hall.

1.1.7.5 Promote the sharing of information and collaborative work between City staff by using the Document Management System, which will allow City staff to access records in an electronic format.

1.1.7.6 Provide an application server that will store and manage required data.

1.1.7.7 Provide and maintain access to data to other City contract providers as necessary.

1.1.7.8 For public records, design storage strategies and systems that are leading industry technology at the time of installation. Implement and coordinate the transfer of data, records, or other materials. as necessary for the operation of the City.

1.1.8 Public Relations

1.1.8.1 Establish a public relations protocol as directed by the City Manager in order to maintain continuous dialog and communications with City residents, vendors and businesses with timely updates.

1.1.8.2 Promote City policy, programs, and achievements by providing communications staff and programs to prepare and distribute various informational data via print, media, and city website-approved messages about the City's progress.

1.1.8.3 Serve as a liaison with residents, civic groups, and other governments, as directed by the City Manager, provided, however, all such activities shall include the disclosure that the Corporation does not have the authority to commit or bind the City without, depending upon the circumstances, the approval of either the City Manager or the Mayor and Council.

1.1.8.4 Document important City events for future use in City-developed publications.

1.1.9 Annual Reports

1.1.9.1 Develop a graphical and thematic design for the Annual Report, subject to the approval by the City Manager.

1.1.9.2 Coordinate with the graphic designers, photographers, editors, and others as necessary.

1.1.9.3 Provide effective written and non-written communications to reflect the year's message and inform residents of the City's actions and achievements per the agreed upon communications plan.

1.1.9.4 Produce and print the annual reports and make available to City residents in hard copy, which may be picked up at City Hall, or electronically in PDF format, which may be downloaded from the City's website.

1.1.10 City Website

1.1.10.1 Design and host the City website, which may contain City contact information, statistics, history, departmental and facility descriptions, the City Council meeting schedule, meeting agendas, agenda packages, minutes, City Codes, notices, pictures, and multimedia. The website will be approved by the City Manager.

1.1.10.2 Update the City website as needed or on a weekly basis to post the latest agendas, packages, minutes, and notices. Redesign the website annually.

1.1.10.3 Publish City-provided geographic information system (GIS) database interface on the website.

1.1.11 City Newsletter

1.1.11.1 Provide text, pictures, graphics, maps, and exhibits as necessary for the quarterly newsletter. The quarterly newsletter will be approved by the City Manager.

1.1.11.2 Coordinate with the publishers to produce a useful, informative, timely and attractive publication.

1.1.11.3 Produce, print, and make available a quality newsletter to City residents.

1.1.12 Program Presentation

1.1.12.1 Publish studies, reports and analysis for staff and public presentation, as directed by the City Manager.

1.1.12.2 Prepare various media presentations of City programs to the staff and general public, as directed by the City Manager.

1.1.13 Information Technologies and Telephone Systems

1.1.13.1 Provide, install, and maintain computerized network system software and hardware that are leading industry technology at the time of installation and sufficient to efficiently satisfy the City's computing needs. The Corporation will develop and implement manual processes sufficient to meet the needs of the City in the Financial Scope of Services (see Section 1.2) prior to (DATE). The implementation of the computerized system will be complete on or about

(DATE), with modules being available before then. The manual processes in support of Section 1.1.14 will also be implemented prior to (DATE), while the computer system to support this function on which the module is based will be implemented on or about (DATE).

1.1.13.2 Provide a domain network that is leading industry technology at the time of installation to handle future growth and technologies. The network system will have limited functions on (DATE). Upon completion of the office space renovations at City Hall, a fully functional system shall be available.

1.1.13.3 Provide, install, configure, and maintain a server at City Hall and the City's offices to improve performance, mitigate against data loss, and minimize potential down time. The server will be leading industry technology at the time of installation.

1.1.13.4 Provide centralized management of network resources and a central location for the storage of the City's documents on site.

1.1.13.5 Assist with maintaining data security and preventing corruption with a nightly backup (with offsite storage) and the ability to restore from a central location.

1.1.13.6 Provide, configure, and maintain__ laptop computers that are leading industry technology at the time of contract inception for the members of the City Council (___), City Manager (__), and City Clerk (__).

1.1.13.7 Provide, install, configure, and maintain up to ________ computer workstations that are leading industry technology at the time of installation for contract and subcontract staff.

1.1.13.8 Provide one digital phone and remote connection for each park site with an office via data line connections that carry both data and voice signal. Provide phone service for the other five existing park sites without offices.

1.1.13.9 Maintain software and hardware uniformity and interchangeability among users.

1.1.13.10 Provide, install, and maintain sufficient network laser printers to efficiently conduct City business.

1.1.13.11 Maintain a 3-year replacement program for computers and equipment.

1.1.13.12 Provide, install, and maintain network cabling/data line system that are leading industry technology at the time of installation for communications, networking, and data sharing.

1.1.13.13 Provide, install, configure, and maintain servers in support of utility functions. Utility servers differ from domain servers in that they are specifically configured to run certain contracted applications.

1.1.13.14Provide City and Corporation with Internet and e-mail connections on a separate server for internal and external communications and common contact lists and scheduling.

1.1.13.15 Archive e-mails in compliance with State retention requirements.

1.1.13.16 Provide, install, and maintain a telephone system that is leading industry technology at the time of installation in City facilities, with sufficient lines and features to satisfy the management needs of the City. The telephone system will have limited functions on (DATE). Upon completion of the office space renovations at City Hall, a fully functional system shall be available.

1.1.14. Databases—Municipal Management Software

1.1.14.1 Provide, install, configure, and maintain a database that is leading industry technology at the time of installation and programmed to manage the City's occupational and business license functions

1.1.14.2 Coordinate the procurement, installation, configuration, and maintenance of databases required of municipalities in the State of Georgia by governmental agencies.

1.1.15 Court Services

1.1.15.1 Provide requested aspects of court record keeping and reporting as required by law and reasonable, sound practices, including, but not limited to, the maintenance of calendars, the recording of sentences and dispositions, the coordination with probation services, and the coordination of collection of fees, fines and surcharges.

1.1.15.2 The Corporation will provide a level of effort consistent with _____ FTE Court Clerk and ____ FTE Assistant Court Clerks for court hearings. The City will provide a Clerk of the Court at City expense.

1.1.15.3 Oversee and maintain systems required for fee, fine, and surcharge accounting, reporting and remittance.

1.1.16 Police

1.1.16 Provide contract administration for police services provided to the City under Inter-Governmental Agreement (IGA) by monitoring and tracking such IGA. After _____ County transition of services to the City on or about (DATE0,

Corporation shall provide clerical and administrative support to a level consistent with _____ FTE, clerks. Such services exclude providing services to input data into the NCIC or GCIC or a similar legally required database.

1.1.17 Fire

1.1.17 Provide contract administration for fire protection services provided to the City under IGA by monitoring and tracking such IGA. After _______County transition of services to the City on or about (DATE), Corporation shall provide clerical and administrative support to a level consistent with two and half ______ FTE, clerks.

1.1.18 Election Support

1.1.18.1 Provide clerical support to the City Clerk's office in coordinating municipal and special elections as required, including, but not limited to, addressing polling station issues, preparing frequently asked ballot questions, or other related issues arising from election clerical support, not including the preparation of ballots.

1.1.19 Solid Waste

1.1.19.1 Administer and coordinate franchise agreements with solid waste providers.

1.2 FINANCIAL SERVICES

Financial services shall include the following:

1.2.1 Revenue Collection

1.2.1.1 Coordinate and liaise with local, state and federal agencies charged with the collection and disbursement of taxes, assessments, fees, charges, and other impositions. To the extent databases delineate Sandy Springs' boundaries, existing tax collection processes and procedures will be used to facilitate timely collection and transfer of revenues to the City. The Corporation is not responsible for the identification and collection of additional revenues from taxpayers and incidents of taxation that are not identified in the existing databases.

1.2.1.2 Administer the existing (and future to the extent that they do not substantially effect the scope of services set out herein) processes, fees, charges, and their miscellaneous revenues pertaining to utilities, private enterprises (for example, business licenses, alcoholic beverage licenses, franchise, and other taxes and fees lawfully enacted by the City) and individuals as they interface with the City programs. This scope assumes the City will adopt the existing or substantially similar fee schedules, methodology, and regulations of ______ County relative to business licenses, alcoholic beverage licenses, and other applicable taxes and fees.

1.2.1.3 Recommend enforcement actions to the City Manager to induce payment in accordance with City and State law and approved policies and procedures.

1.2.1.4 Prepare monthly financial reports showing revenues and expenses to date in comparison with budget projections and submit the reports to the City Manager no later than the tenth day of the following month.

1.2.1.5 Maintain the existing and future address list and database for the City and State Departments of Revenue to assist the City with obtaining local and shared revenues.

1.2.1.6 This scope does not include the cost analysis and fee modeling required to establish and collect regulatory fees pursuant to (STATUTE).

1.2.2 Capital Program Administration

1.2.2.1 Coordinate the capital needs of the City with the designated City representatives. Capital Program Administration means providing coordination and recommendation to the City on an annual basis as to the capital program requirements in future years, which includes the scheduling of capital program projects. Both Parties agree that Corporation's duties under this Agreement are limited to the coordination for capital improvement programs and procurement and program management for small projects (i.e., estimated procurement contract value of under $_____ although final decision will be based upon the complexity of said project), unless otherwise agreed upon between the Parties. Corporation's duties do not include the program management of the large or complex (those projects outside of the above definition of small projects) which would be outside the Scope of Services herein and, accordingly, handled through an additional services authorization and change to the Agreement as per Section 9.2 of this Agreement.

1.2.2.2 As directed by the City Manager, advise and assist the City in obtaining financing if necessary and maintain proper fund accounting procedures.

1.2.2.3 As directed by the City Manager, formulate recommendations and provide resources to administer and implement the City's approved capital program financing.

1.2.3 Investment Services

1.2.3.1 Assist the City in the development of investment policies and procedures pursuant to Government Finance Officers Association of America (GFOA) and State law.

1.2.3.2 Assist the City in selecting an investment firm that will invest City Funds at the direction of City Manager and in accordance with GFOA policies and State law.

1.2.3.3 Produce investment reports, including cash flow analysis and modeling stating the effectiveness of the chosen investment policy, on a quarterly basis.

1.2.4 Fund Accounting

1.2.4.1 Develop and implement a Fund Accounting System in accordance with Governmental Accounting Standards Board (GASB), the Uniform Accounting System prescribed by Department of Community Affairs, and the rules of the (STATE) Department of Audits and Accounts.

1.2.4.2 Prepare reports in accordance with reasonable and customary City reporting standards for Department of Community Affairs and State Revenue Department and distribute in a format to be agreed upon between the parties.

1.2.4.3 Prepare monthly management reports and other financial reports as required by applicable law and accounting standards.

1.2.5 Accounts Payable/Receivable

1.2.5.1 Administer the purchase order system such that timely payment of invoices will be made on behalf of the City, provided the necessary funds are made available by the City.

1.2.5.2 Coordinate tax collection, franchise fees, utility taxes, and other receivables.

1.2.6 General Fixed Asset Accounting

1.2.6.1 Account for assets constructed by or donated to the City for maintenance.

1.2.6.2 Within the first twenty-four (24) months from contract execution, inventory City property in accordance with GASB and the (STATE) Department of Audits and Accounts.

1.2.7 Budgeting

1.2.7.1 Prepare and submit annual budgets per GFOA standards to the City Manager.

1.2.7.2 Coordinate with and assist City departments for annual budget preparation and presentation.

1.2.7.3 Provide material for and attend required budget meetings, hearings, and agenda meetings.

1.2.7.4 Coordinate the budgeting function between City departments and other governmental entities as necessary.

1.2.7.5 Present the City approved budgetary information to appropriate parties as requested and in accordance with City approval in oral, print, multimedia, and web-based forms.

1.2.8 Forecasting

1.2.8.1 Prepare detailed financial forecasts and analysis in a format to be agreed upon between the parties.

1.2.8.2 Identify trends and analyze their impact upon the City's finances, operations, and capital, and advise the city of such findings.

1.2.8.3 Provide data and assist with the development of policy and action recommendations.

1.2.8.4 Coordinate the forecasting function with and/or between City departments and other governmental entities.

1.2.8.5 Present findings in oral, print, multimedia, and web-based forms to the City.

1.2.9 Comprehensive Annual Financial Report (CAFR)

1.2.9.1 Prepare the Annual Financial Report for Units of Local Government in accordance with Generally Accepted Accounting Principles as defined by the _FOA.

1.2.10 Risk Management

1.2.10.1 Work in conjunction with City-designated insurance broker regarding claims to City's insurance policies and with recommending and advising the City of the appropriate amounts and types of insurance and work with insurance broker to procure the necessary insurance as directed by the City Manager.

1.2.10.2 Assist in the processing of claims at the direction of the City Attorney and the City-designated insurance broker.

1.2.10.3 Develop and maintain a risk management claims review procedure in coordination with the City Manager, the City Attorney, and the City-designated insurance broker.

1.2.10.4 Review insurance policies and coverage amounts of City vendors.

1.2.11 Human Resources

1.2.11.1 Maintain databases and documents to assist in the proper functioning of employment services, payroll, fringe benefit, insurance, tax, and other City-specific and general law-provided human resources functions.

1.2.11.2 Develop and implement a Code of Conduct for personnel that emphasizes the responsibility of the staff to be professional, patient, and responsive. The Code should emphasize that rudeness and impoliteness toward any person is unacceptable conduct and will not be tolerated.

1.2.11.3 Develop and implement with employees an Employee Policies and Procedures Manual, which shall include, but not be limited to, policies and procedures on carrying out duties to the City, consequences of non-compliance to policies, and functions and roles of the employees.

1.2.12 Purchasing

1.2.12.1 Recommend to the City Manager, for approval by Mayor and City Council, and assist in the implementation of, approved procurement policies and procedures consistent with State and local laws, rules, and regulations.

1.2.12.2 Consistent with approved policies and procedures assist in selection of vendors.

1.2.12.3 Participate in county and State level purchase plans when determined to be in the best interests of the City and as directed by City Manager.

1.2.12.4 Prepare Request for Proposals to be distributed to vendors and suppliers as directed by the City Manager.

1.2.12.5 Prepare and process purchase requisitions.

1.2.13 Health Insurance Portability and Accountability Act of 1966 (HIPAA)

1.2.13.1 Review and make recommendations regarding City systems and procedures to meet the requirements of HIPAA.

3.2 Facilities Maintenance, Repair and Contracts

3.2.1 Provide a level of effort consistent with _____ FTE personnel to maintain, repair, clean, and keep in good working order City Hall facilities commensurate with local governmental standards, which shall include, but not be limited to, such services as janitorial services, painting services, and minor repair of equipment. However, this provision shall not apply to landscaping maintenance of City rights-of-way or land. The structural, mechanical, electric, and plumbing facility maintenance for all City facilities is not included in the scope.

3.2.2 The Corporation will implement a Computerized Maintenance Management System that will allow for the generation of work orders to track and schedule maintenance activities in this scope of services. The manual procedures in support of the scheduling of maintenance will be place on (date). Modules will be implemented in phases until _____(date). Full implementation will be completed on or around ________.

3.3 Furniture, Fixtures, Equipment and Supplies

3.3.1 Provide furniture, fixtures, equipment, and supplies in an amount not to exceed one hundred and fifty thousand dollars ($150,000.00) for the term of this Agreement for the reasonable operation of departments and functions of the City.

2.2.2 Title to such furniture, fixtures, equipment, and supplies shall vest in the City upon purchase by Corporation on behalf of City. All leases shall be in the name of Corporation and shall include an assignability clause to the City.

2.2.3 All software purchased by the Corporation on behalf of City shall be licensed appropriately under the name of the City.

4.0 PURCHASING, PROCUREMENT AND CONTRACTING

4.1 The Corporation shall comply with applicable laws and requirements regarding purchasing and procurement as set forth by the State of _______. The Corporation shall comply with applicable laws and requirements regarding contracting required in the course of fulfilling the duties under this Agreement as set forth by the State of _______ _____________.

5.0 PUBLIC WORKS

5.1 Public Works services shall include staffing and maintaining the Public Works Department for the City. The areas of responsibility shall include the following:

5.1.1 Stormwater

5.1.1.1 Under the direction of the City, coordinate with other City personnel and/or contractors for the assumption, maintenance, storage, and retrieval of available documents and records that are necessary for the effective implementation and operation of the City's stormwater requirements under applicable, federal, state, and local laws. The City shall facilitate the transfer of records. The Corporation shall be responsible for determining the documentation necessary for transfer, as well as coordinating and implementing the physical retrieval, reproduction, and storage of the transferred records.

5.1.1.2 Provide ongoing engineering, design and maintenance for the operation of stormwater system, as needed, to meet the needs of the City per Section 3.3 of the Agreement. Scope of services is limited to daily maintenance. Other services such as master planning and design services for capital program shall be handled per Section 3.3 of the Agreement.

5.1.1.3 Develop and recommend to the City and upon approval implement the necessary policies, protocols, rules, and regulations to meet or exceed the City's stormwater requirements under applicable federal, state, and local laws, including, but not limited to, federal clean water requirements.

5.1.1.4 Integrate activities as necessary with Planning, Zoning and other departments by establishing department head planning sessions that incorporate integrated client service goals.

5.1.1.5To accomplish the stormwater services, the Corporation will provide the following levels of effort with reasonable municipal management practices:

a. Furnish a level of effort consistent with 50 percent of one FTE position during startup and two FTEs ongoing for records transfer.

b. Furnish a level of effort consistent with 25 percent of one FTE for stormwater design.

c. Furnish a level of effort consistent with a crew of three FTE for stormwater maintenance.

d. Furnish a level of effort consistent with 25 percent of one FTE for policy development.

5.1.1.6 The scope does not include water sample collection, environmental testing, or reporting.

5.1.2 Emergency Preparedness

5.1.2.1 Develop and recommend policies and guidelines to the City, and upon approval, coordinate, operate, and maintain the City's emergency preparedness program in accordance with applicable federal, state, and local laws, as well as prudent local government practices.

5.1.2.2 Integrate and coordinate emergency preparedness operations in conjunction with Homeland Security, Emergency 911, Federal Emergency Management Agency (FEMA), and (STATE) Emergency Management Agency.

5.1.2.3 To accomplish emergency preparedness the corporation will provide:

a. Baseline safety audit during transition
b. Recommended Emergency Preparedness Plan (EPP) policy during transition
c. Practice exercise during transition
d. Up to $___________ for emergency cleanup (annually).

151.3 Recycling

5.1.3.1 Prepare and recommend policies and guidelines to the City, and operate the City's recycling program or a similar recycling program (up to $______ annually).

5.1.3.2 Upon adoption, coordinate implementation of program and other activities with City personnel and/or contractors.

5.1.3.3 Fulfill reporting duties as required by applicable federal, state and local laws.

5.1.3.4 This scope of service does not include the hauling or disposing of yard waste or hazardous substances.

5.1.4 Geographic Information System (GIS)

5.1.4.1 Coordinate with the necessary City personnel and/or contractors for the assumption, maintenance, storage, and retrieval of available documents and records that are necessary for the effective implementation and operation of the City's geographic information system (GIS) database. The Corporation shall be responsible for determining the documentation necessary for transfer, as well as coordinating and implementing the physical retrieval, reproduction, and storage of the transferred records. Core elements of the GIS database will be in place to allow City staff to store and access GIS files and data obtained from ______ County. The full implementation of the GIS database and interfaces will be complete on or around _______..

5.1.4.2 Service, update, and maintain GIS databases on not less than a monthly basis.

5.1.4.3 Provide GIS-related information and/or data in response to requests and needs of City personnel.

5.1.4.4 To provide GIS services, the Corporation will provide levels of effort consistent with _____ FTE during startup and ___ FTEs for ongoing operations.

6.0 TRANSPORTATION

2.1 At the direction of the City, the transportation services shall include establishing, staffing, and maintaining the Transportation Department for the City. The areas of responsibility shall include the following:

6.1.1 Funding and Grant Applications

6.1.1.1 Conduct activities necessary to identify, develop, and prepare submissions for federal, state or local funding and grant programs, and provide fund oversight as required by law. Coordinate those aspects of the above, as necessary with the ______ Regional Commission and other local governmental entities as may be necessary. To accomplish the above service, Corporation will provide a level of effort consistent with __ percent of a Transportation Planning Manager and __ percent of a transportation planner.

6.1.2 Traffic Engineering

6.1.2.1 Conduct operational activities (maintenance, engineering, and planning services) necessary to maintain a traffic system, including conducting necessary studies and implementing traffic control improvements. To accomplish these services, the Corporation will provide a level of effort consistent with ______ FTEs under the direction of the Transportation Director, which includes up to $______ for the first year (20__) of traffic system operations and improvements, which includes street striping and signage. Design services for capital program projects and consulting services for master planning are not included in this scope of services and shall be handled per Section 4.3 of the Agreement.

6.1.2.2 The scope does not include the purchase of Christmas decorations for the City.

6.1.3 Street Design

6.1.3.1 Conduct activities necessary to maintain a street system plan, including the coordination, review, and management of contracts for streets, sidewalks, and related projects. To accomplish these services, the Corporation will provide a level of effort consistent with __ percent of one road engineer. In addition, in order to manage ongoing Capital Improvement Plan (CIP) projects, the Corporation will provide a level of effort consistent with __ percent of one CIP manager and ___ CIP engineer.

6.1.4 Street Maintenance

6.1.4.1 Conduct activities necessary to maintain a roadway and bridge infrastructure system, including minor repairs, pothole repairs, cleaning, and minor repairs necessitated by storm events. At City request, Corporation may perform utility cuts to the roadway which will be repaired and inspected as per City specifications by the Corporation. Corporation may also perform, at the direction of the City, the non normal road and bridge repair (such as wash outs, sink holes and damage caused by vehicle accidents). The utility cuts and non normal repairs are not included within this Scope of Services and shall be handled as per Section 8.2 of the Agreement. In order to accomplish this service, a baseline condition of streets will need to be obtained and updated by the Corporation. The Corporation will then put into place a preventive and corrective maintenance system and a capital program list will be developed and prioritized for the City Council. For these services, the Corporation will provide a level of effort consistent with ____ FTEs and maintenance sub-contractors. The scope does not include costs to procure, operate, or maintain street sweeping services or resurfacing City streets.

6.1.5 Street lights, Sidewalks, Gutters and Related Street Areas

6.1.5.1 Conduct activities necessary to maintain street lights, sidewalks, gutters, and related street areas.

7.0 STREETS, RIGHTS-OF-WAY, AND FACILITIES

7.1 General

7.1.1 Streets, rights-of-way, and facilities services shall.

7.1.1.1 Coordinate the identification of City rights-of-way. The Corporation shall be responsible for determining the documentation necessary for future needs.

7.1.1.2 Operate and oversee aspects of the City rights-of-way permitting process. Right-of-way permits are issued for curb-cuts and private use of the City-owned rights-of-way. To accomplish this process, the Corporation will provide a level of effort consistent with _____ FTE and maintenance sub-contractors.

7.1.1.3 The Corporation shall be responsible for up to $____ per event and up to $_____ per year invested in the planting and maintenance of City rights-of-way beautification.

7.1.1.4 The Corporation shall not be responsible for security at City facilities, including both staff and security apparatuses such as metal detectors.

7.1.1.5 The scope includes up to $_______ for street light electricity. The Corporation shall not be responsible for other utility costs associated with facilities, streets, or rights-of-way, including, but not limited to, water and electricity other than noted here and in Section 8.1.1.

7.2 Contract Administration

7.2.1 Operate and oversee aspects of contract administration for the daily maintenance of public rights-of-way and property, including landscaping and irrigation systems, in order to provide safe and comfortable common grounds for the residents of (CITY). The scope includes hiring a subcontractor, scheduling, inspecting contracted work, and reviewing and approving payment requests.

7.2.2 Operate and oversee aspects of contract administration for the construction (excluding CIP; refer to Section 4.3 of

Agreement)), operation, and maintenance of public facilities. The scope includes hiring a subcontractor, scheduling, inspecting contracted work, and reviewing and approving payment requests.

7.2.3 Operate and oversee aspects of the emergency preparedness plan for debris removal, roadway access, flood prevention, and safe, operable utilities. To accomplish this service, the Corporation will provide the elements listed in Section 5.1.2.3. The scope includes preparing the plan, setting up a practice session, distributing a contact list, and reviewing and implementing (STATE) and FEMA requirements through Corporation employees and subcontractors, with local, state and federal agencies.

8.0 PARKS AND RECREATION

8.1 Parks and recreation services shall include staffing and maintaining the Parks and Recreation Department for the City. The areas of responsibility shall reasonably include the following:

8.1.1 Plan, recommend, and upon adoption, implement and coordinate staffing and contract administration for the daily maintenance and use of public parks and recreational facilities. The scope includes managing and procuring the services of subcontractors and temporary personnel on behalf of the City to administer recreation programs and manage subcontractors performing maintenance functions such as mowing, fence repair, and ballpark lining. The scope includes electrical costs of up to $240,000 for the lighting of the ballparks and associated fields.

8.1.2 Plan, recommend, and upon adoption, implement and coordinate staffing for the planning, promoting, and supervising of recreation programs and special events. Special events include festivals and parades but not field trips. The Corporation shall set up traffic barricades and provide cleanup services after an event is over, for up to two City events per year. The Corporation shall not provide security or transportation services for programs or events.

8.1.3 Plan, recommend, and upon adoption, implement and coordinate staffing for the managing, coordinating and scheduling of City athletic facilities, as needed. The Corporation shall set up traffic barricades and provide cleanup services after an event is over. The Corporation shall not provide security or transportation services for programs or events.

8.1.4 Develop and recommend to the City Manager short-, mid-, and long-range plans for capital improvements and implement the plans as directed by the City Manager. The scope does not include the development of a Park and Recreation Master Plan by the Corporation.

8.1.5 Operate and oversee aspects of emergency management procedures with local, state and federal agencies. To accomplish this service, the Corporation will provide those the elements listed in Section 5.1.2.3.

8.1.6 Conduct the activities necessary to identify, develop, and prepare submissions for federal, state or local funding and grant programs for improvements to the park and recreation system within Sandy Springs and provide fund oversight as required by law.

8.1.7 To accomplish the parks and recreation services, the Corporation will provide a level of effort consistent with ___ _ FTEs, plus subcontractors, for programs and maintenance under the direction of the Parks and Recreation Director.

8.1.8 Under no circumstances shall the Corporation be directly involved in the distribution or sale of alcoholic beverages.

9.0 CAPITAL IMPROVEMENTS

9.1 Develop and recommend short-, mid-, and long-range plans for capital improvements and implement plans as directed by the City Manager. The plans should meet the requirements of the Department of Community Affairs and the (AREA or REGION) for adoption in the City's Comprehensive Land Use Plan. The Corporation has allotted a level of effort consistent with __ percent of each of the following Director's positions to accomplish this service: Community Development, Public Works, Transportation, and Parks & Recreation, with support of one full-time planner and __ full-time administrative assistant split between these areas. This scope of service does not include procurement services for the capital improvements, which will be handled per Section 4.3 of the Agreement.

10.0 PLANNING AND ZONING

10.1 Planning and zoning services shall include staffing as needed to meet the requirements herein and operating the Planning and Zoning Department for the City. The areas of responsibility shall include the following:

10.1.1 At the direction of the City, provide information to the general public as it relates to land development activities within the City.

10.1.2 At the direction of the City, provide information to builders and developers regarding policies and procedures related to land planning within the City.

10.1.3 Oversee the development, maintenance, and updating of land use and zoning maps as approved and required by State and local agencies.

10.1.4 Prepare and recommend policies and procedures regarding planning and zoning activities and prepare and recommend schedules and time frames for processing land development activities, including, but not limited to, zoning.

10.1.5 Provide information to the City Manager, Mayor, City Council, Planning and Zoning Boards, and other City entities needing information regarding relevant and applicable zoning and/or planning issues.

10.1.6 Develop and recommend a plan for the implementation and assessment of impact fees by the City. Upon adoption, implement the plan in coordination with City staff and/or contractors. The scope does not include an impact fee study.

10.1.7 Conduct activities necessary to maintain a planning and zoning system for the City. These include, but are not limited to, the following:

a. Receiving, processing, and approving building plans
b. Building inspection

c. Recommend enforcement of codes including signs, landscape, and arborist

d. Preparing a comprehensive plan, including zoning ordinances
e. Reviewing land development plans
f. Inspecting land disturbances

10.1.8 Develop and recommend a plan for the issuance of certificates of use and certificates of occupancy (COs). Upon approval, implement the pan in coordination with other City staff or contractors.

10.1.9 To accomplish the planning and zoning services, the Corporation will provide a level of effort consistent with __ ___ FTEs under the direction of one full-time Community Development Director.

11.0 INSPECTIONS, CODE ENFORCEMENT, AND PERMITTING

11.1 Inspections, code enforcement, and permitting services shall include staffing and operating the inspections, code enforcement, and permitting functions for the City. The areas of responsibility shall include the following:

11.1.1 Develop and recommend a plan for the review and inspection process for the City. Upon adoption, implement the plan in coordination with City staff or contractors.

11.1.2 Develop and recommend a plan for the building permit and inspection process for the City. Upon adoption, implement the plan in coordination with City staff or contractors.

11.1.3 Develop and recommend a plan for the code enforcement process for the City. Upon adoption, implement the plan in coordination with City staff or contractors.

11.1.4 Develop and recommend a plan for the City to conduct Soil Erosion and Sedimentation Control inspections. Upon adoption, implement the plan in coordination with City staff or contractors.

11.1.5 To accomplish the inspections, code enforcement, and permitting services, the Corporation will supply a level of effort consistent with _______ FTEs in Code Enforcement and ___ FTEs, plus sub-contracting inspection services, in Permitting and Inspections under the direction of one full-time Community Development Director.

CPSIA information can be obtained at www.ICGtesting.com
Printed in the USA
236668LV00001B/44/P